Beautiful
BONSAI

Beautiful BONSAI

Bruno Delmer

Photographs by Jacques Boulay

STERLING PUBLISHING CO., INC.

NEW YORK

Contents

A Tree First and Foremost

Can anyone resist the fascination of a bonsai? Can anyone not stop in wonder at the sight of such a perfect tiny tree? The harmony that flows from it and the balance of its proportions create an impression of wholeness. Stronger still is a sense of the tree's vitality: aged, venerable, it can fit in the palm of your hand—yet it blooms, bears fruit, then sheds its leaves.

Literally, the word bonsai means "tree in a pot." More charmingly, it symbolizes the cultivation of a tree in a container. A bonsai is thus a reduction, a model tree. This is not to say it is a dwarf tree. To prove it, one need only replant it in the ground: very quickly, nature reclaims it and the tree grows to its normal size.

Most trees fade into the forest. We notice among them only the very old or very majestic. Bonsai on the other hand, cannot fail to arouse our deepest curiosity—if not our amazement—regardless of their shape or size. Their size lends them another aspect: it magnifies all the species' unique characteristics. The specimen has been minutely considered to achieve a certain

A Japanese garden at the end of the nineteenth century. All the elements are in harmony, and nothing is left to chance; nature is tamed, pruned, mastered, sublimated.

The Pleasure of Bonsai

A Scale Model of Nature

Inspiration from nature is the very essence of bonsai.

The Chinese, who first conceived the idea of growing a scale model of nature in a container, were doubtless inspired by the exceptional forms of trees high in the mountains, distorted and twisted by wind, cold, and snow. They took upon themselves not only the difficulty of uprooting a tree from its rock but that of keeping it alive. Over time, a technique of "miniaturization" was thus devised, and by around the year 800, the practice of putting "trees in pots" was already very popular in China.

appearance. The artful fashioning and sculpting of the young plant over a period of years produces a model of its full-size counterpart that belies its diminutiveness. It is more than a mere tree; it is the embodiment of the perfect tree. It is the paradigm and glory of its species.

Introduced there by a Chinese diplomat, this concept of cultivation encountered great success in Japan: the aristocracy, monks, and artists quickly embraced it. In the hands of the Japanese, the intuitive process gradually became a very precise and demanding art—it is the rules they imposed that still determine the success of a bonsai today. In the Meiji Period (1868-1912), this technique of cultivation reached its peak of popularity (the "invention" of copper wire at that time reducing to a few moments the shaping of the tree that had previously taken several seasons with hemp string) and spread into every level of society. Today, the art of bonsai is most closely associated with Japan.

The small size of their land mass has determined the relationship of the Japanese with nature—a profound respect tempered by a need to dominate.

A Life Linked to Nature

If the Japanese brought the art of bonsai to its height, it is perhaps because the relationship they have with nature is particularly deep and enduring. The brief blooming of the cherries calls for giant picnics out under the trees. Long lines of visitors to the national parks accompany the bloom of the water iris. Even the Japanese cuisine is tied closely to the seasons: the chestnut crop and the plum tree in blossom are traditionally celebrated with pastries; young eels in spring and the harvest of the first rice in autumn are the inspiration for celebrated seasonal dishes.

The Japanese live very close to nature, for though they have managed to make habitable a good portion of their mountainous archipelago, they live there at the mercy of the elements: earthquakes, tsunamis and typhoons are fairly common. This relationship with nature is inverted in their gardens, in miniature. Nothing is left untouched: everything is pruned, tamed, and shaped. By tradition, every growing

How big is a bonsai?

Naturally, the very word bonsai signifies that it is small. But what exactly is the size range of these plants?
The Japanese have answered this question by establishing a classification system in which bonsai are presented by category in national exhibits. A bonsai falls into the miniature tree category when its size does not exceed 8.5 inches (21 centimeters) from crown to neck (where it meets the earth). A bonsai is said to be medium when it measures up to 20 inches (50 centimeters). Over that, the tree enters the category of large bonsai, of a size that requires the effort of two people to move.
The Chinese do not rely on this type of classification. For them, the bonsai is something else—a tree cultivated in a pot in the courtyard of a house, not on a shelf inside. This explains why their bonsai are by tradition comparatively large.
A novice may easily confuse the large Chinese bonsai and the Hueki, *potted trees of a similar size. In this case, not only the technique, but the goal, is different: the latter are destined to be planted in the ground, in gardens. Even a slightly trained eye will recognize the species used to this end: generally the holly with small, evergreen leaves,* Pinus Pentaphylla *and* Juniperus chinensis

thing is tailored, be it an azalea or a cedar tree. Accordingly, the arrival of autumn brings the "plucking" of the black pines; the leaves are removed just before they become brown and fall. This labor-intensive process causes an enormous influx of volunteers to temples, palace squares, and imperial villas throughout Japan. Dressed all in white, they enjoy tremendous honor participating in the imperial grandeur of this ceremony and working for the good of nature. The bonsai is nothing less than a scale model of this well-tended nature.

[Learning by Looking]

Familiarizing yourself with bonsai as a work of art requires that you take the time to examine it. The beauty of a bonsai obeys extremely precise rules that determine its quality without compromising its character, its charm. It is not rare in Japan to see auction bids climb dizzyingly for a bonsai, which, despite its flaws, expresses an undeniable grace.

The best school "for developing an eye" for bonsai, besides visiting bonsai exhibitions often, is to look at the largest number possible of fine books containing photographs of trees. It was thus by observation that, around the twelfth century (the Kamakura period), the Japanese, having long since become masters of the art, elaborated the principles that govern the cultivation of bonsai as we practice it in the West. China, Thailand and Vietnam still take many liberties in their treatment of bonsai.

The Trunk

The silvery beech bark is utterly smooth, almost like white powder. The bark of the Japanese maple is an aged gray color, slightly cracked; that of the *Stewartia,* a cousin of the *Camellia,* bears a beautiful orange tint…and each is like an invitation to touch it. All trees have bark that is visually interesting, but a bonsai's bark is also testament to its age. A bonsai faced with so cracked a bark can hardly be mistaken as young. Even if age is not essential either to their beauty or their worth, nevertheless, it contributes greatly to the veneration that surrounds bonsai.

The trunk, more or less thick depending on the style of the tree, always grows slowly thinner from the soil level to the crown, without any major blemishes or wounds that could render it without value. Bonsai

The root of this trident maple literally hugs its support to become one with it.

exhibits and auctions traditionally take place in winter, when the leaves have fallen, making all the tree's flaws visible.

Unlike the Chinese, the Japanese consider blemishes objectionable—and consequently, so do western enthusiasts. The filler they have thus developed to camouflage them is perfect: applied to wounds of a sixteenth of an inch (3 millimeters) and larger, it falls off by itself as soon as the scar is formed. The scar is not necessarily considered a flaw, but it must not draw undue attention by being immediately visible. It is, moreover, one of the reasons why the majority of bonsai have sinuous trunks.

The Branches: The Architecture of the Tree

Ideally, every tree should be inscribed in a triangle, more or less high, flat or pointed, of which the different points are defined by the top of the bonsai, the extremity of the main branch and the edge of the second most important branch. Thus the tree represents the union of three fundamental elements: Heaven, Earth, and Humanity, source of beauty. The topmost branch symbolizes Heaven. The lowest branch symbolizes Earth, and the line determined by the second branch, Humanity. This principle guides the overall shaping of the bonsai; it applies as well to the Japanese art of cut flowers, ikebana.

A branch must always appear at the extremity of a curve in the trunk, towards the outside. It cannot appear in the front, for example, if it originates in the back of the tree. In other words, the branch must not cut across the middle of the tree. Its growth must appear natural. Though it may seem otherwise, its site does not result from chance, but from subtle endeavor.

Seen from the front, a tree stripped of its leaves resembles a fish skeleton, the trunk being the spine, and the branches, the ribs—rather like a spiral staircase. Each branch is selected for its appropriate position. Thus, the most important, or main, branch must be situated at a 90° angle in relation to an axis defined by the bonsai and the gaze of an enthusiast, whether seen to the left or the right. The second branch (branch number two) must be situated opposite it, at a 45° angle to the bonsai-spectator axis. Branch number three must come above the main branch, at a 40° or 30° angle, without being face on, however. The prescribed configuration of the branches con-

Thirty years of attentive care…and all of 7.5 inches (19 centimeters) high! They say "the best things come in small packages," and this Japanese maple is a case in point.

tinues thus. Ideally, the most forward facing branch comes at the first third of the tree's height, while the first branch to be totally toward the rear comes between the main branch and the second branch. The distribution of the limbs overall confers a sense of balance, once the positions of the main and the second branches are defined.

The head of the tree, be it the main branch or the tuft of needles that finishes the crown, must always project toward the spectator. The sap rises first to the top of the tree, which is consequently the fastest growing part. Thus, in order to maintain the proper appearance, the unsightly summit must be trimmed for the benefit of the small neighboring branch, which will be the head in its turn.

The Surface Roots

A bonsai whose roots range evenly around its trunk, except for a crucial space in front, creating the ideal perspective...the dream of every bonsai enthusiast.

Only the trident maple, or *Acer berguerianum*, a particularly amenable species, has surface roots that, in time, create a true plateau. More often, bonsai need encouragement to develop a pleasing set of surface roots. Diverse techniques have been developed for this purpose, including propagating plantlets from cuttings from such species as the pine and the *Zelkova*.

A very beautiful example of surface roots on this *Stewartia monadelpha*: the roots are harmoniously arranged in a star shape around the trunk.

Green Pea Bonsai

The Japanese have created a very special, but somewhat marginal, bonsai size classification called Mame *which literally means "green pea bonsai." The name pretty much describes the tree: it ranges from one to three thimbles. An entire collection of these could sit in the palm of your hand!*

The Leaves, a Peerless Pleasure

A maple's flamboyant red spring shoots, the *Ginkgo biloba's* golden leaves of autumn. What heartwarming satisfaction to witness the changing colors of the leaves over the course of the seasons. The spectacle comes, once again, not by chance, but by regular and careful pruning.

Pruning to reduce the size of the foliage is a fairly simple process, but not all species readily lend themselves to it. Trees with naturally small leaves or needles, such as the elm, the hornbeam, and the five needle pine, are easily managed—not so the plane tree

(American sycamore—*platanus sp.*) or the catalpa. Understandably enough, these trees are never used as bonsai.

Pretty foliage is a long-term pleasure, and when a leaf becomes yellow or gets a spot, it can even provide a measure of drama. But whereas a yellowed leaf on a tree several feet tall may go unnoticed, on a several-inch high bonsai, it takes on the air of an ecological catastrophe.

The Forms

Broadly speaking, there are as many forms as there are trees, since no two trees are identical. Nevertheless, the Japanese—in manipulating nature, in idealizing and classifying it—have ordained a certain number of accepted forms. Descriptions of the most common follow, introducing some of the vocabulary unique to bonsai cultivation.

These shapes are determined by the angle that the crown of the tree assumes in relation to its trunk. As they grow, trees adopt all angles, from the strictly upright to the acute, in which the head of the tree cascades below the top of the pot.

According to the tree's natural inclination

As bonsai, the trees take the shape into which you train them. From *Hokidachi* ("broom style") to *Chokkan* ("formal upright") to *Shakan* ("windswept")—the choices are vast. From left to right: a *Pinus pentaphylla* in the *Moyogi* (informal upright) shape, a *Zelkova serrata* in the *Hokidachi* shape, and two Japanese maples, also pruned in the *Moyogi* shape

and inherent qualities, it will be fashioned, like a sort of "modeling clay," into an idealized representation of nature (this is the Japanese school), or a mythological representation (in the Thai or Chinese school).

Formal upright or *Chokkan*—Pines and cryptomerias best lend themselves to this shape, as well as *Juniperus chinensis* or *rigida*. It is exactly the form of the cedar in nature: straight, majestic, with a thick solid trunk, and branches curving under the weight of the years. The very thing that

makes it the ideal image of "the Tree" is also what makes it so rarely used: it requires a straight perfect trunk, devoid of flaws. The layout of the branches rarely permits this.

Broom style or *Hokidachi*—This form irresistibly evokes a broom stuck in the ground upside-down, and the Japanese gray-bark elm (*Zelkova serrata*) is the only species which nature and the Japanese bonsai canon allow to assume it. With its very thin branches and very small leaves, the *Zelkova* is transformed in less than five years into a beautiful "broom" bonsai. Pruned regularly to prevent the branches from growing to the detriment of the foliage, and "tied up" in a bundle all winter so that it is "re-compacted," it easily maintains its pleasing shape.

Informal upright or *Moyogi*—This is the form most often used, being suitable for all species. It makes very pleasing bonsai with sinuous trunks with more or less accented curves. This shape easily allows you to reduce the height of a young plant when you shape it, and thanks to the sinuous nature of the truck, to mask the inevitable scar caused by removal of the "sacrifice branch" (a branch grown to increase trunk girth and later cut off, leaving a wound). Remember that all the branches should start from the outside of the curve, i.e., no branch should cut across the middle of the tree.

Slanting or *Shakan*, and windswept or *Fukinagashi*—The major difference between these two is that *Shakan* possesses branches which are shaped by the wind's force, while *Fukinagashi* has no branches at all, the wind's force having obliterated them. The pines, notably the *Pinus pentaphylla* (Japanese white pine) and the five-needle pine, work best in this style and are especially beloved by the Japanese. Some broad-leafed trees, such as the Chinese elm, produce equally satisfying results. An important element is the pot, which must be flat enough to go virtually unnoticed, so as to give maximum effect to the wind blowing through the tree.

Cascade or *Kengai*—Along with the broom style, this form is the most popular with the public and bonsai enthusiasts alike. The form abounds in nature, on the edges of cliffs and the steep sides of mountains.

Though all sorts of variations exist, the chief characteristic is that head of the tree falls below the level of the ground. The least qualification is that the whole of the bonsai reside outside the axis of the container and the head of the tree rest in the void. It is imperative that the volume of the pot correspond to the mass of the foliage to counterbalance its center of gravity. With this in mind, be sure to tie the pot down on the shelf to avoid its tipping or blowing over. Most species are pretty accepting of this

Semi-cascade or windswept? A little of both perhaps, but what power in this tree only 6 inches (15 centimeters) high!

Have you ever held a tree in your hand? This one makes it possible—it's 12 inches (30 centimeters) of pure harmony.

Detail of the creation of trunks in a small wood of tropical elms in the "raft" style.

shape, but be realistic. A pine, a juniper, or a box tree can be trained this way, but an apple tree cannot. As unlikely as this shape might seem for a bonsai, how much more so for a tree in nature.

Group planting or *Yose-ue*—As the name implies, this category has the appearance of a small wood or miniature forest. The challenge here is to respect the rules for planting the trees in the dish, which must be very flat. To give the impression of some depth, it is necessary to understand and employ perspective, and to vary the heights of the trees so as to make each one visible. Another shape that simulates a grove is cultivated from the branches of a tree whose trunk has been completely buried.

Here again, we encounter the essential triangle. The forest is organized around a pivot tree, planted at a spot a third of the way from the edge of the pot's length. Matching this placement, to its left or right, comes its counterpart, tree number two, slightly shorter and thinner than the first. The third tree is situated just slightly behind the pivot tree; smaller and thinner than the first two, this already creates an illusion of depth. All the others are placed in the background, generally an odd number of trees between five and seven, which grow progressively shorter and thinner.

The species best adapted to this shape are the beech, the hornbeam, and the maple, and small-needled conifers such as the juniper and the yew.

Exposed roots or *Neagari*—This form is not very often used for species of temperate or cold climates which tend to insulate their roots underground. The winter jasmine and the quince however are exceptions which allow you to emphasize their roots. It is principally the tropical species that are most apt to have exposed roots. So it is with the *Ficus*, for example. This is its natural growth habit, and the more exposed roots it has, the more interesting the tree will be. One of the cardinal rules in cultivating bonsai is to capitalize on and magnify the qualities unique to the species.

A comprehensive list of all the recognized bonsai shapes is too large to include here. One other, however, deserves mention—*Ishitsuki*, which suggests a tree growing directly on a rock, or gripping a rock tightly in its roots before they plunge into the ground. The object is not the multiplicity of choices, but the satisfaction of training the tree to a shape that best suits its natural tendencies. This is the real pleasure of bonsai.

Witnessing Nature Through the Seasons

The first bonsai to arrive in Europe came from the Land of the Rising Sun, where conditions made it possible for them to adapt without undue stress.

People in other Asian countries—China, Taiwan, Vietnam, Korea, even Thailand—cultivate trees in pots as well. These countries cover a vast area and an extensive range of climatic conditions, and certain species, which thrive there in the open air, are unable to develop fully elsewhere, except indoors, under controlled conditions.

Accordingly, it is advisable to distinguish the outdoor from the indoor bonsai of tropical origins, because they require different care. The pleasure they provide is nevertheless of equal intensity.

THE COMING OF SPRING. The days grow longer, the temperature rises, and nature is in its glory. The first buds begin to peer above ground, and the potted trees begin to lean toward the full sunlight (but beware of late freezes). The winter jasmine and the quince are the first to bloom. Then the apple, plum, and hawthorn in turn enchant us. Why not do as the Japanese and bring them indoors to enjoy their beauty all the more! This is the time for pollinating fruit trees. Trees indoors being especially isolated from natural pollinators such as bees, it is critical for the grower to perform this essential task.

February and March, before the bloom, call for the repotting of flower and fruit trees; for the others, the mild days and cool nights of spring are conducive to the rapid renewal of roots before the onset of the sultry heat of May and June.

The rising sap manifests a wild exuberance as new shoots start up in every direction. But be forewarned: this luxuriant vitality can begin to upset the balance of the bonsai. Pruning is imperative!

As the buds grow, their need for careful watering intensifies. The plants must be watered vigilantly, sometimes twice a day, until the leaves have taken on their adult texture. Should it be hot, as it can sometimes be at the end of spring, do not hesitate to mist them (but, of course, never in full sunlight!).

Indoors, spring is equally perceptible. The days become longer and the need for artificial light lessens. The heater is less often used and the air becomes less dry, so watering can be less frequent.

Spring....rising sap, delicate buds, irresistible vitality!

The first shoots make their appearance and the flowering trees come into their own, *Carmona* and *Serissa* first. The rapid spring growth can quickly give a bonsai a wild appearance. The Chinese elm, the *Sageretia theezans*, the *Carmona microphylla* the *Serissa foetida* will not balk at being pruned, and frequently!

Repot them around April or May. Indoor bonsai may require repotting much less often because they do not lose all of their leaves. Be careful, as always, to turn the trees regularly in front of the light source, so that they make a complete turn every week. This advice applies equally to indoor plants and to those on balconies or terraces. At the appearance of the first spring shoots, fertilize and begin to water thoroughly and regularly.

THE SUMMER, for outdoor bonsai, begins fairly early, with the first big heat waves. After several successive warm days, the trees must be put in the shade. Light shade very often proves sufficient for pines, quinces, jasmines, hawthorns, ivy, and others that are fairly tolerant of sun. By the same token, the more sensitive maples, beeches, hornbeams, junipers, apples and plums will appreciate more protection.

Watch the tree's water needs very carefully. Check your trees daily. They may sometimes need to be watered twice a day. This may be your only worry, but it is a consid-

A Taiwanese evergreen cousin of the wisteria, the *Millettia reticulata*.

Age has no price

As paradoxical as it may seem, age plays almost no part in the market value of a bonsai, for the weight of years does not necessarily imply perfection. A very old tree can be less beautiful and therefore, less valuable, than a young but perfect tree. The bonsai craze in the western world has supported intense and rapid production to answer demand, very often to the detriment of quality Trees that have a complete "genealogical" file are rare. In fact, only those of the imperial collection in Tokyo have a complete recor enabling us to ascertain that they were sown more than four hundred fifty years ago.

The care that you give your trees is always generously repaid. In summer, sumptuous flowers reward precise watering.

compensated for by the splendor of their flowers.

Summer is a rather tranquil season in terms of care, except for watering. The major pre-occupations are enjoying the sight of your trees, planning the work for fall, checking the wiring and keeping alert to the smallest sign of an enemy presence—scale, gray and red spider mites, and aphids.

erable one. A healthy, well-established tree should be thirsty at fairly regular periods, on average every day.

After their extravagant blooming, you may want to set aside wisteria and plum trees. Their wilted foliage, of a size nearly as big as their full size counterparts, can be rather unsightly. But this "too shall pass," largely

All indoor plants profit from a good summer stay in the garden. The rain, the wind, and the variations in temperature from day to night give them a good "vacation." Acclimation to the new conditions—more light, more sun—must be done progressively. The *Ficus*, for example, requires one to two weeks to be able to withstand the sun. And then each has its particular demands. The

elm likes direct sunlight, as does *Murraya*, while *Carmona* prefers the more gentle rays of morning or late afternoon.

The major hazard for indoor bonsai "on vacation" outdoors is the lack of atmospheric humidity. A good practice is to put the pot in the shade, over bricks set on a plate full of water. And regular misting discourages attack by spider mites.

AUTUMN is truly the season of raptures, in which you reap the fruits of your labor. When the maple and the beech begin to don hues of golden yellow, deepening to orange-red, they arouse a certain ecstasy. The thrill of this spectacle never lessens, however many years you are privileged to see it. Some diehard bonsai lovers even put off business trips to savor this exceptional moment.

If the season is mild and without strong squalls, the fall color can last up to three weeks. But an early cold wave or a small November storm is enough to end it. Happily, the memory remains.

Just as in the wild, "forests" of beech may sometimes harbor mushrooms. And like the hornbeam, they offer marcescent foliage in the winter, (i.e., they do not fully shed their leaves). Just the same, it is best to remove the remaining dry leaves so as to inspect the boughs. Apple trees and quinces are covered with fruit, but beware the voracious birds!

The Japanese hold that applying solid fertilizer until the end of summer (some time between the end of August and mid-September), just before the leaves begin to turn yellow, greatly encourages the growth of the trunk without harming the thinness of the boughs. This is also the only time, when the needles have achieved their full size, that pines need to be fertilized.

Tropical trees do not experience seasons as well defined as do their counterparts in temperate regions, even if the attentive bonsai lover perceives the more vigorous shoots or notes the appearance of flowers on a *Carmona* or a *Murraya paniculata*. The fall, for indoor bonsai, is simply the signal of a return to indoor heat. But as long as relative temperatures inside and out are not too different, they can remain outside. At the same time, it is imperative to re-acclimate them indoors before turning on the heater. To assure the welfare of bonsai over the winter, be careful to follow these important steps: refill the plates underneath with water; turn the plants regularly in front of the window; mist them; stop all fertilizing; remove the residual solids that may be left on the soil; verify that garden or balcony parasites have not followed them inside; and for caution's sake, treat all new plants that enter the house preventively, whatever their origin.

Whatever its size, a tree is still a tree. Whether in a garden in Kyoto (above) or a bonsai collection in Paris (opposite), the colors of autumn are resplendent.

An autumn walk through a bonsai nursery (above) transports you to a magical "world of the senses." Plunge into the colors of autumn, but keep a cool head and buy your bonsai in the winter—the tree unveils itself completely then and allows you to make a more informed decision (below).

IT IS IN THE WINTER in Japan that all the exhibits and auctions for bonsai take place. (Keep in mind that this is summer in the Northern hemisphere.) Devoid of leaves, the trees are bare in all their beauty. It is easy then to judge the quality of the tree and the skill of its cultivator. For the same reason, this is also the season for structural pruning.

Under your attentive, even amorous gaze, the bonsai is fully revealed; it is the only time of year when the tree's essential form is laid bare. The tree can be contemplated as a block of clay to model—to fashion to your ideal, your wishes—and new ideas can germinate. But winter is sufficiently long to allow for judicious consideration. Decisions need not be made in haste. Should there be any doubt, you must return the bonsai to its place and wait…for once the branch is cut, it cannot be reattached.

In any case, your first consideration is to put winter safeguards in place. The broad-leafed trees, having lost their leaves, can remain in some darkness. Be careful of

moss that thrives in this condition too; it might cause the tree to rot and blacken. Evergreens and semi-evergreens, like privet, must receive some daylight. The ideal is a frame—a little greenhouse facing north—to allow the light but prevent the sun from raising the temperature and causing early breaking of the trees. Fall and early winter are also good times to reshape conifers, as the needles are in repose, and to remove old wires before they scar the branches.

The lack of light in winter is but one danger that outdoor bonsai face: another very real one is a lack of water. They can die of thirst in the heart of winter, for watering can be a challenge with the threat of hard freezes. Trees vary in their need for water: broad-leafed trees are often less thirsty than conifers or the boxwood, for example. For all trees, however, you must put to use the slightest thaw: at least check to confirm that your trees are not dry, and water them as needed. Equally important is to open up the "greenhouse" when the weather is fair; outdoor bonsai endure considerable hardship, generally being open-air trees in nature, having to remain shut in for two or three months at a time. An additional benefit here is that increased air circulation prevents all sorts of rot caused by the plants' confinement.

A Source of Happiness

Some bonsai lovers readily admit that their bonsai are like their children, being totally dependent on them. This is a big responsibility and a daily source of happiness. A tender young shoot, a flowering bud, the colors of autumn, bare boughs in winter—small things that add up to enormous pleasure. Even the simplest of chores, like watering, is a chance to enjoy your tree.

Tropical trees sheltered indoors face minimal risk unless exterior doors are carelessly left open, or even purposely left so to air out the room following a smoky dinner. They will not appreciate it, and they will let you know, either by wilting (*Carmona* or *Serissa*), by producing spotted leaves (*Sageretia*), or by young shoots turning black (*Ficus*).

To avoid the stress of rapidly changing temperatures, be sure to move the bonsai to another room while you are airing out the place. Watch out for accumulating dust, as well. Mist the trees often—you might even to give them a "shower" once a week in the bathtub. The oversize leaves of the *Ficus* can be wiped with a damp cloth.

Dryness in the atmosphere is a real threat to the welfare of your plants. Bonsai should be set in a large plate, resting on a layer of sand, gravel or expanded clay marbles, and this layer should be kept moist. Artificial lighting is a nice supplement because these plants enjoy ten to twelve hours of light daily in their natural habitat. By giving them the equivalent artificially, you will prevent the yellowing and untimely falling of the leaves. Gradually as the days lengthen, you should treat them to sun in the morning and late afternoon and avoid the sun at midday, unless your home is very dark.

What follows are brief introductions to some of the many species commonly trained as bonsai. Further discussion will familiarize you with the techniques of bonsai cultivation and help you understand the passion of those who practice them.

In Peking, the flower market also offers bonsai wrapped up and ready to go.

Broad-
Leafed
Trees

[Fire Red
Corollas!]

The quince offers an explosion of simple, small red flowers with delicate yellow stamens. It is often still very cold, with days that hardly rise above freezing, while the other trees remain dormant, when this wild-looking little bush bursts into irrepressible bloom. This tree blooms so early that people sometimes miss it! Fortunately, it blooms a little again in the summer and sometimes in the fall.

You might be tempted to try an amusing little experiment while the tree is in bloom. See if you can pollinate some flowers and grow a quince. They are small—about the size of a plum—and inedible, but very fragrant.

If you manage to produce some fruit, be very careful with it. Move the tree smoothly, with the utmost care, or you risk knocking off the fruits that are not solidly fixed.

A nursery worker tradition

When a young bonsai nursery worker sets up shop, the custom is that he begin by putting some Chaenomeles speciosa cuttings in the ground to produce quickly a stock of readily salable trees. The habit of this plant is to grow very long, fairly thick roots, which give rise to new shoots—it makes a lot of suckers. So to create a small bonsai quickly, you need only cut the sucker at its base and repot it.

Free form for two species

Two species are especially often shaped as bonsai: *Chaenomeles japonica* and *Chaenomeles speciosa*. The former is often planted in gardens where its unique blooming adorns it with very large pink, red or white flowers. It has a smooth, fairly thick trunk. It is easy to prune and propagate by cuttings, and it can also be shaped with no problem. Perhaps its only flaw resides in its large and slightly soft leaves. It is ideal to cultivate in a miniature forest shape or bush, with multiple trunks, in free form—as opposed to straight and classic, as it never has this appearance in nature. These extremely popular trees are put in very colorful pots and sold in the spring when in bloom. They generally finish the summer in the far end of the garden.

The second, *Chaenomeles speciosa*, has a very different charm. Its leaves are much smaller—green and shiny—and its trunk is thin, with a rapidly cracked bark that quickly gives it an aged look. It produces smaller flowers with a vibrant red more intense than *Chaenomeles japonica*, and it can have a repeat flowering. It is very often cultivated in free form, as a bush, at full size. It is a tree that grows naturally as a bonsai and that the Japanese love a lot and use often.

Common name:
Japanese quince tree
Latin name:
Chaenomeles speciosa
Age: *25 years old*
Size: *15 in (35 cm)*
Shape: *Moyogi*
Outdoor
Origin: *Japan*
Collection: *Rémy Samson*

Sun for one, shade for the other

Chaenomeles speciosa loves the sun. In fact, leaving it in the sun at the height of summer will encourage a good bloom. Be vigilant, though, because it must get only a little bit dry between watering.

Chaenomeles japonica, on the contrary, prefers to remain in the shade on the hottest days of summer, its foliage being more fragile. It must not dry out much at all between watering.

These two species must be very carefully fed from May to October. Prune them both after the bloom and during the season in order to keep their balanced shape.

Ideally, quince trees should be repotted between the end of summer and the beginning of autumn so that they have time to grow strong roots before winter. Be mindful that they are very subject to attack by gray and red spider mites.

Chaenomeles japonica, like its cousin *Chaenomeles speciosa,* has very brittle wood. Use copper wire covered with paper or raffia and tie it very gently.

A favorite in Japan

Cydonia sinensis or *Pseudocydonia sinensis* is the tree that produces quinces. This true quince tree is characterized by a smooth, dark brown trunk, with large leaves of a fairly light green color, and a bright pink bloom followed by enormous fruit, which make it a much appreciated and very popular bonsai in Japan. But it is rarely encountered outside Japan because it is not easy to deal with: its delicate formation and brittle wood make it work only as a very large subject. Furthermore, it requires constant attention because its branches and trunk grow very quickly, and they are easily scarred by the wires.

Common name: *Japanese quince tree*
Latin name: *Chaenomeles japonica*
Age: *25/30 years old*
Size: *16 in (40 cm)*
Shape: *Yose-ue*
Outdoor
Origin: *Japan*
Collection: *Rémy Samson*

Winter Jasmine

Bouquets of Golden Stars

Common name:
Winter jasmine
Latin name:
Jasminum nudiflorum
Age: *15 years old*
Size: *8 in (20 cm)*
Shape: *Ishitsuki*
Outdoor
Origin: *Japan*
Collection:
Japanese

A cracked, knotty, ochre trunk supporting very dark green branches capped with lovely golden yellow flowers: this is the winter jasmine. More a groundcover than a bush, it is the first plant to bloom, announcing the imminent end of winter. This is a welcome harbinger and gratifyingly longlasting, as the flowers succeed each other for something close to two weeks. Large stems covered with buds are sometimes cut from the garden and brought inside to force the bloom. Jasmine bonsai are frequently forced this way in Japan, where central heat is uncommon and the plant is not subjected to great variations in temperature. You can do the same thing by placing your bonsai in the warmth beside a window. Avoid burning from direct sunlight, though, and remove it quickly once it has wilted.

In summer, the jasmine's fairly small, dark green foliage gives it great charm.

Strange shapes

Unlike *Jasminum nudiflorum, Jasminum officinale* is extremely unsuitable for cultivation as a bonsai, because it forms almost no wood (except on very old plants), so it is very soft. The winter jasmine, on the other hand, is very often treated as a small to medium bonsai. It is easy to cultivate and lends itself well to the more unusual shapes: cascade, semi-cascade, even *Moyogi*. But be careful: this vigorous creeper should be pruned very often to keep its desired shape.

It likes the sun

To encourage short internodes and a good bloom, the winter jasmine must remain in full sunlight all year. Remember to prune its overgrown shoots very regularly, especially after it blooms, but leave some of them until the end of summer: it is these which will bear flowers the following spring. Water it a lot, but allow it to dry out a little, and feed it very carefully from May to October. Wiring is the only real difficulty with this plant. To give the jasmine a shape, you must be careful to wire the branches only when they are very tender, after making it slightly thirsty, so as not to risk breaking the extremely straight wood. But since it responds well to pruning and enjoys vigorous growth, any possible mistake will be quickly corrected.

Repot the plant after it blooms and before the leaves begin to fall. At that time, feel free to cut its incredible, very compact, ochre yellow rootlets: they re-grow at such speed that it is advisable to repot the plant at least every two years.

A Rite of Spring

Common name:
Cherry tree
Latin name: *Prunus cerasifera*
Age: *50/60 years old*
Size: *16 in (40 cm)*
Shape: *Raft or forest*
Outdoor
Origin: *Japan*
Collection: *Japanese*

This tree is the very symbol of Japan. Its flowering signals the arrival of spring, and it is tradition to picnic then under the cherry trees, on grass covered in petals. But a storm or a gust of wind is enough to sweep away the spring magic. Luckily, the bonsai cherry can be sheltered from intemperate weather, making it possible to savor the bloom longer.

A cherry tree without cherries

There was a time when the Japanese searched the more remote regions to find and collect trees "tortured" by the elements, shaped by the harsh effects of lightning, wind, and cold. These "dramatic" shapes appeared all the more extraordinary in contrast with the pure and charming bloom of a variety such as the *Prunus mume*. Trees in the wild are now protected and their digging up is prohibited.

The quest of bonsai professionals remains, however, to produce such fabulous trees, and numerous species—pines, junipers, plums—yield excellent results. So it is with the cherry tree, though in this instance, it will not produce fruit, because the only varieties cultivatable as bonsai are flowering ones.

In summer, after it blooms, you may want to put the cherry tree aside because, like the wisteria, its outsize leaves dwarf the small tree and look a little incongruous.

Be daring with the pots

Trees of this type, like plum trees (*prunus*) in general, are particularly suited to a wealth of colors and shapes in the choice of pots. It would be a real shame to limit your choices here, since bonsai so much more often demand discretion. Even among discriminating collectors and in museums, you find trees of this type in pots decorated with pastoral scenes, flowers and abstract designs that mix perfectly with the tree's exuberant bloom.

Simple maintenance

Give it regular care. As with all blooming trees, repot it every two years in a slightly enriched mixture with a little added compost just before it blooms, or in the fall if you are able to protect it from the extremes of winter. Choose a spot where it will get a lot of light, sun and air, but be sheltered from the burning rays of the summer sun. Prune the tree after it blooms. Because its boughs are fairly thick, try to wire it when it is "green," that is, when the shoots are still very young and tender. This may entail letting it dry out a little to make it supple. Be careful, the wood is very brittle. If the cherry tree has not been repotted, don't forget a good autumn fertilizing.

The Wisteria

[A Fragrant Cascade]

This very vigorous creeper is inexpressibly sumptuous in bloom and the silvery gray sheen of its soft bark invites the touch. Take any opportunity you can to see it at least once in your life. In winter, take advantage of its bareness to appreciate its simple architecture.

The wisteria bears two types of buds: the pointed, which will make leaves, and the "round" which will transform into flowers. Little by little the flowers will multiply. The first clusters form, their color deepens, and the flowers spread out. These clusters of flowers largely surpass the plant in size, which for this reason is almost always treated in the semi-cascade style—all the better for you to enjoy its fragrant blossoms. Naturally, the wisteria must be carefully protected from wind, rain and harsh sunlight during this period.

This type of plant should be treated as a bonsai of 20 to 28 inches (50 to 70 centimeters) in height, in pots of sufficient depth and size to limit the effects of the wind.

Common name:
Wisteria
Latin name: *Wisteria sinensis*
Age: *40 years old*
Size: *20 in (50 cm)*
Shape: *Moyogi*
Outdoor
Origin: *France*
Collection: *Rémy Samson*

A true savage

Once the wisteria wilts, it is better to place it out of sight in a corner of the garden because it will then rediscover the momentum of a wild plant. Its foliage is immense and its growth is messy. All the same, it is important to let it grow like this all summer if you want it to be full of flowers again next season. If the branches become too full and begin to invade its neighbors' space, a little pruning from time to time will not harm it. But serious pruning must take place in the fall. Shape the plant by keeping only the branches that will bear flowers. Pruning for shape is done right at the beginning, when you decide to treat the plant as a bonsai. At that time, the bloom is much less important than the overall shape of the tree. Wiring should be done after it blooms. Use only aluminum wire covered well with raffia or thin synthetic moss; you will thus prevent all marks. The tree's trunk and branches grow very rapidly, and an oversight can happen....

This insatiable legume needs to be repotted yearly after it blooms, and fed very carefully from May to October. Placed in full sunlight it will assure you of a beautiful bloom, though you will be contending with sizable foliage and frequent copious watering.

[A Symbol of Immortality]

Common name:
Plum tree
Latin name:
Prunus subhirtella 'Autumnalis'
Age: *8 years old*
Size: *11 in (28 cm)*
Shape: *Moyogi*
Outdoor
Origin: *France*
Collection: *Rémy Samson*

In terms of bonsai, the plum covers all trees of the genre *Prunus* (almonds, peaches, plums), cultivated uniquely for their bloom. These trees bear pink or white flowers whose simplicity and purity offer a marvelous contrast with the very black trunk and rough bark, a perfect union of fragile grace and virility. It is clear enough how the plum tree flower came to symbolize immortality in China and Japan. Understandably, the plum is chiefly cultivated and sold in spring, and is associated with the pine and the bamboo, which are likewise highly symbolic. These decorative hotpots are offered as good luck charms. In this case, of course, the quality of the tree is secondary to the beauty of its flowers.

The *Prunus subhirtella* "Autumnalis" is sometimes treated as a bonsai. This variety of *Prunus* flowers in autumn, giving numerous very small flowers of pale pink, full of freshness and delicacy.

Difficult to treat as a bonsai

The plum tree is fairly difficult to treat as a bonsai because its wood is very brittle. You must take care to wire the wood when green and allow it to get thirsty beforehand to make it supple. It produces a small number of very long shoots, with equally long internodes. These require pruning, but not too much because the flowers appear only on the wood from the year before.

Sometimes, despite all your attentive care, the branches on an older tree may die for no apparent reason. This is the nature of the tree; it bears no reflection on you. Just be forewarned, so you do not panic needlessly.

The plum is yet another of those trees whose foliage is of a size that does not always give the best effect after it blooms, so it is best put aside. The majority of plum trees come from *Yama-dori* ("collecting in forests"). You have certainly seen such trees in nature. Their general size is quite imposing—let alone their cracked, twisted, hollowed-out trunks—perhaps even a little much for a medium bonsai. Imagine the challenge of trying to keep one of these alive after it is transplanted.

Good sun treatment

This is a species that needs a lot of sun, even in the summer—but be vigilant during the burning hours of July and August. Good sun encourages the development of the floral buds in August while limiting the growth of the internodes.

As always, water thoroughly, but let it dry out a bit between watering. From June to October, apply solid fertilizer. Repot each year when the tree is young, then only every other year when it matures. It is rare for bonsai plum trees to produce fruit.

Accentuate the contrast of its very dark bark and pale bloom by planting your tree in a vibrantly colored pot. Do not be afraid to go a little wild.

The Hawthorn

[Simple Happiness]

Common name:
Hawthorn
Latin name:
Crataegus oxyacantha
Age: *50 years old*
Size: *22 in (55 cm)*
Shape: *Moyogi*
Outdoor
Origin: *France*
Collection: *Rémy Samson*

The Hawthorn, or *Crataegus*, is a marvelous bush that grows everywhere like a weed. Its very fragrant, off-white bouquets have the serene charm of simple unpretentious plants. Its leaves are naturally small and it blooms easily, if not particularly early. If you can guarantee its pollination, *Crataegus* will produce fruit just as easily.

Silver until a certain age, the trunk in time will crack, which gives the plant the air of a respectable old lady. Its branches are thorny, but not to the point of wounding the cultivator. Autumn is its best season: it is cloaked then in sumptuous hues of orange, rust, and yellow. Imagine all the colors…and fruit too! But beware of blackbirds. They too are taken with this tree and it is their pleasure to devour the fruit.

In the informal upright shape

Its very robust growth makes the hawthorn an especially easy bonsai to work with. The shape that most suits it is the *Moyogi*, or informal upright, which makes the most of the "bush from a wild hedge" aspect of this very natural tree. One sometimes sees quite beautiful specimens with knotty old trunks from which a part of the bark seems to have been torn off by the wind, and the trunk cracked by the cold, wind and time.

Easy to live with

This tree enjoys full sun, but its tender foliage can still suffer unsightly burns from too much exposure.

It likes water just as much, but you must let it dry out a little to keep its foliage fairly condensed. As with most fruit trees, it is advisable to repot it each year when the tree is young and when it is mature, every two years. If the hawthorn still does not bloom, treat it like a normal broad-leafed tree, and treat it regularly with bonsai fertilizer.

Serious pruning presents the only real problem with this tree: its strong growth has a tendency to produce great numbers of shoots which, without skillful trimming, risk transforming into inextricable "knots."

These can come to resemble arthritic knuckles and can grow as thick as the trunk itself! The only alternative is to cut before shaping a branch with aluminum wire. The trunk itself does not grow very quickly, so be patient until you see it thicken. The hawthorn has a precious advantage over many other species: it is easy to obtain. The pink variety will give you equally good results if you can find a plant grafted at the base.

Common name:
Hawthorn
Latin name:
Crataegus oxyacantha
Age: *16 years old*
Size: *7 in (18 cm)*
Shape: *Moyogi*
Outdoor
Origin: *France*
Collection: *Bruno Delmer*

Welcome to Paradise

In every season, the apple tree is a beauty, but its bloom alone is ample reason to include one in your collection. Once the fruit forms—and you must help because bees cannot do it all in the city—the waiting begins. First, you see the pistil grow, then you anticipate the harvest. This is when the tree is most vulnerable to fickle weather; it must be carefully watched over because a fruit that fails to make it to term is a tragedy. Children are often fascinated by this tree, making it a fun introduction to bonsai.

Apple picking...or not

As for chores, the summer is easy. You may allow the tree to become a little dry, though watch out that it never lacks for water. Drying out can cause the apples to rot and fall. Aside from that, leave it in the shade, not exposed directly to the sun. From the end of its bloom until the harvest, feed it appropriately. Then in fall, it will offer colored foliage as well as mature fruit. For the varieties with small fruit (*Malus halliana* x 'Everest' or

An apple as big as a tree...

...or is it a tree as small as an apple? It is possible for a miniature bonsai to bear an apple as big as the tree itself. This is a variety with very large fruit, and it is imperative that the roots be allowed to "dig deep." Water and nutrition must be sufficient and regular enough for them to see the tree through to the successful completion of its mission.

'Perpetua'), it is better to leave the apples in place without gathering them until the following spring. On the other hand, with those varieties bearing very large fruit, it is better to gather them so as to prevent their wearing out the tree, which could compromise production the following year.

Common name:
Apple tree
Latin name: *Malus
cerasifera*
Age: 35 years old
Size: *24 in (60 cm)
long, 16 in (40 cm)
high*
Shape: *Shakan*
Outdoor
Origin: *Japan*
Collection: *Rémy
Samson*

Two schools of repotting

Repotting can be done either in October or just before the tree buds. The disciples of the October cycle feel that in spring the humidity is not sufficient for the tree to root well and that it will not be strong enough to flower, let alone to bear fruit.

The others, those who do the work in spring, believe that repotting in October leaves the root system vulnerable just as winter comes. Experience shows that annual repotting, done fairly early before the tree buds, gives the tree exactly enough time to root well before blooming. And since an early or rigorous winter can never be ruled out, it is better to repot in the spring.

Maintenance pruning shortens the leggy spring shoots, insuring that the tree keeps its shape throughout the spring and summer.

The lushness of the apple tree allows a lot of leeway in the selection of a planter. Let your imagination run wild. The opportunity for this kind of small pleasure is rare enough.

The Elm

Majesty!

Common name: *Elm*
Latin name: *Ulmus parvifolia*
Age: *13 years old*
Size: *2.5 in (6 cm) high, 7 in (18 cm) long*
Shape: *Semi-cascade*
Outdoor
Origin: *France*
Collection: *Bruno Delmer*

This species is nearly ideal for becoming acquainted with the art of bonsai. It is a beautiful and majestic tree that graced parks and neighborhoods across the country before Dutch elm disease decimated it. It grows quickly and fairly straight, and is recognizable by its imposing posture. Its leaves are naturally small, its thin branches spread out easily, and its trunk thickens with no trouble. The slightly shiny, tender green foliage takes on the superb colors of rust and golden yellow at the end of autumn. Add to this autumnal palette the carpet of moss that covers the pot…and the spectacle nearly equals nature's grandeur in the forest.

Subtropical climate or real winter

It is necessary to distinguish the so-called Chinese elm from the European elms (which have smaller leaves), even if the two have the same name: *Ulmus parvifolia*. The first, *Serissa* and *Carmona*, enjoy the heat of a subtropical climate. The second, on the other hand, have a resolute need to endure a real winter. Similar in appearance, they

Sowing the seed...of art

It is a special privilege to work with children to familiarize them, even the very young, with the cultivation of bonsai. By helping you, they very quickly pick up the knowledge and the passion, and it will soon become their own. Let them start by helping you water the plants. Once they get a feel for it, assign them a small tree. You can begin with a very easy species, like the Chinese elm (indoor or outdoor bonsai), the Ficus retusa (indoor bonsai) or the trident maple (outdoor bonsai). These three species grow rapidly and can become very presentable bonsai within three years. For a marvelous gift, offer your child a tree that you began raising at his birth. In time, the little bud will become a bonsai, growing along with your child until he finally takes over its care. What a great legacy to leave a fortunate child...and a much-loved bonsai. It is no small matter to create a tree. It is an adventure that can last beyond your lifetime.

This Chinese elm, about forty years old, measures 30 inches (80 centimeters) and belongs to the collection of Mr. Phung.

differ from one another chiefly in their bark: it is smoother—even as a mature tree—and silvery gray on the tropical elm. The foliage of the tropical elm will also be more compact and the leaves thicker and shinier.

Pruning endlessly

This outdoor elm (*Ulmus parvifolia*) is an Asian species. It prefers a lot of light, but avoid full sunlight in the hottest hours, as with the majority of broad-leafed trees. Water it thoroughly but, as with most outdoor trees, let it dry out a little between watering. Its vigorous growth makes a supply of solid fertilizer indispensable.

This energetic grower will produce young shoots throughout the summer, and even into fairly late fall, until just before the leaves turn yellow. Consequently, you must prune it very regularly, to one or two leaves, so that it keeps its shape—and especially so that the heart of the foliage itself will not suffer for the sake of the outer edges.

Growth at such a pace is not without effect on the wiring. Wiring not carefully monitored can very quickly compress the limbs, permanently marking the bark. The most popular shape remains definitively the formal upright, which gives this magnificent tree its commanding presence.

In Japan, professionals generally choose to plant this species in unglazed clay pots, which bring out the brilliant green of the foliage. As the bark of the tree cracks with age, the dark environment magnifies its beauty.

It likes it outdoors as well as in

Another variety, the tropical elm, has the advantage of being able to adapt as an outdoor or indoor bonsai. If you grow it outdoors all year, it can withstand temperatures as low as 10°F (-12°C), when well protected. In this case, place the tree in full sunlight to encourage healthy and compact foliage, and allow it to dry out a little more between watering. Its fertilizer and pruning needs are identical to those of its Asian counterpart.

Always plan ahead, where possible, for repotting outdoor trees. Repot before the bloom. A tree cultivated indoors should be placed in a very well heated room, preferably in front of a window facing east. Turn it regularly so that it receives equal light on all sides and grows symmetrically. Like the majority of indoor bonsai, it will thrive on a plate filled with moist gravel, sand or expanded clay marbles; this provides humidity that will discourage spider mites, which prefer a dryer atmosphere. Spider mites suck the sap from the leaves, causing them to discolor. The leaves will fade and, on the undersides, you will see the whitish, cobwebby signs of their colonies. Should they appear, you must treat the bonsai immediately with a product made specifically for them. If the problem persists, change the product: spider mites adapt to a pesticide very quickly.

Common name: *Elm*
Latin name: *Ulmus parvifolia*
Age: *60/70 years old*
Size: *36 in (90 cm)*
Shape: *Moyogi*
Indoor
Origin: *China*
Collection: *Mr. Phung*

Common name: *Chinese elm*
Latin name: *Ulmus parvifolia*
Age: *60/70 years old*
Size: *34 in (85 cm)*
Shape: *Forest*
Indoor
Origin: *China*
Collection: *Mr. Phung*

The Siberian Elm

[Grand Elegance]

Imagine the tree as temptress! An apt metaphor for this elm: it truly holds a special place in the hearts of bonsai enthusiasts everywhere. Almost always treated in the broom style, it is the epitome of bonsai: a model tree. This image is so pervasive that it very often serves as a kind of pictogram for bonsai.

In Japan, the tree lines avenues. It is very tall and slender, with a straight and silvery trunk bearing spongy lens-shaped spots, which are its pores. Its long thin branches, which irresistibly evoke a straw broom turned upside down, carry very light foliage, barely enough to provide a gentle shade. Its leaves are small, long and somewhat jagged, and they take on warm colors in autumn: golden yellow and then orange before becoming rusty. It preserves these qualities as a bonsai. They say of this tree as they do of all others in the Land of the Rising Sun: of a hundred seeds that sprout, only ten will yield pretty trees, and of a single one, a tree that is sublime.

A technique which calls for careful handling

Once the seed has germinated, the root is cut more or less a half an inch (one centimeter) from the cotyledon (i.e., the first pair of rudimentary leaves that appears after germination). The truth is, the Japanese create a seedling. They practice—on pines as well—a very tricky technique, which requires careful handling and stringent hygiene and humidity. The object is to guarantee from the start the most beautiful surface roots possible. A first selection is carried out, and only about twenty seedlings, those having roots arranged in a star around the trunk, make the cut. The next step is to stimulate the branches by pinching back the head of the young shoot as soon as it reaches the required size, about one-third the height of the future tree. Again, the selection process is severe: the branches must be thin—none thicker than the others—and arranged in the proper pattern. In the end, the most beautiful of these bonsai fetch astronomical sums at auction.

The other 80 or 90 trees that do not meet these exceptional criteria will be treated in either the broom style or the forest. Such is the lot of those that fall short: they are not sufficiently beautiful to stand alone, but are perfect for a charming composition of very pretty trees.

Neither too much nor too little water

Whether your *Zelkova* is your own creation of that of a professional, you must now provide for it. Place it in the sun in spring and fall; in summer, it will need a little shade. Watch that it is watered well and is not allowed to suffer thirst or over-watering. The appearance of black spots on the leaves is a clear symptom of necrosis. Should this occur, cut back the affected leaves to induce new shoots. Feed it regularly from May to the end of October. Prune it routinely, like all elms, however, keep one leaf per shoot because *Zelkova* grows new leaves very quickly. On an adult tree in good health, you can strip the leaves yearly, if necessary. It will produce leaves more proportional to its size.

A pot in keeping with the trunk

Zelkova must always be planted in a very flat glazed container larger than the shadow made by the tree's boughs, and of a depth corresponding to the trunk's thickness. A mature specimen should be repotted every three or four years before the buds open. Leave the tree in the shade until its first leaves appear.

Common name: *Siberian elm*
Latin name: *Zelkova serrata*
Age: *30 years old*
Size: *4.5 in (11 cm)*
Shape: *Chokkan*
Outdoor
Origin: *Japan*
Collection: *Bruno Delmer*

Age: *18/20 years old*
Size: *12 in (30 cm)*
Shape: *Chokkan*
Outdoor
Origin: *Japan*
Collection: *Rémy Samson*

Photo page 52

The Essence of Japan

Veneration best describes the regard in which the Japanese hold this tree. Its lightness, grace, and delicacy make it not only a beautiful garden subject, but a superb bonsai. In spring, tender shoots appear, ranging from pink to almost red, and then give way to very green leaves. Its growth is so vigorous that the long powerful shoots it sends out can grow up to 14 inches (35 centimeters) in a few weeks, even in bonsai.

Subtle shades of autumn

In the summer, with proper pruning, its foliage flutters enchantingly at the pleasure of the wind. For a little while, you can almost imagine yourself at the other end of the world, lying on a thick carpet of moss under its light boughs.

Autumn is certainly its season. Very early, it is adorned with a multitude of colors. The palette is infinite: a single maple can bear subtle tints of red, orange, gold, yellow and even violet. The season's rapture can be prolonged indefinitely, provided the weather is hot, but not excessively, the nights mild, and the wind fairly still. The beauty of fall is splendid reward for the labors of summer. The only regret is not having more maples.

Viewing stones: *Sui-seki*

In the Shinto religion, each being, each object, has a "soul," and stones likewise have importance. The Ryoan-ji garden in Kyoto is the epitome of this: the stones and raked sand there invite meditation. In Japan, collecting stones is more than a pastime; it is a veritable passion supported by an active industry. Just as with bonsai, the inspiration comes from the Chinese, who have begun to pay steadily increasing prices for stones evoking fantastic mountains, waves, and animals.

The enthusiastic Japanese entrust an artist to fabricate a very flat custom base in wood, which perfectly follows the contour of the stone. The size of the stone varies, just like bonsai, from a few to as much as 16 or 20 inches (40 or 50 centimeters).

Collectors display these stones on shelves on their wood bases, or on bonsai plates of ceramic or bronze, on a layer of very fine sand. Outdoors, they are arranged in groups on trays or plates of water, which in summer evoke the tranquility of a cooling stream. There is the story of an emperor who so loved his Sui-seki that he was never without it. His favorite stone accompanied him everywhere, carried on a cushion in its own little box! Truth or legend, it doesn't matter. This is merely evidence of the passion that the Japanese bring to the art of stones.

This art is often paired with that of bonsai, Sui-seki appearing frequently in bonsai presentations at exhibits. Literally, Sui-seki means "water stone," because the majority of them come from streambeds or shores. In principle, a stone of quality must be in its natural condition, unchanged in any way by man. The standard is becomingly increasingly important as Sui-seki have now begun to circulate in the West. At the very least, a good stone must be verified not to have been cut from its base. Its beauty, certainly, would not be lessened in this case, but its value would be compromised considerably in the eyes of the enthusiast.

It prefers the shade

It is the duty of every bonsai lover to have an *Acer palmatum* in his collection. This is a relatively carefree tree that appreciates the shade, as full sunlight and dry wind in the summer can burn the tips of its leaves. It should be misted regularly, morning and night, and allowed to dry relatively little between watering. Take special care in watering, though: just as with too little water, an excess harms its leaves. It should be repotted every three years, and fed regularly from May to October.

Forced to make leaves

The only real problem with this species is getting it to make small leaves. Its spring growth is so violent that the first leaves appear on a stem of only three-quarters of an inch to a little over an inch (2 to 3 centimeters). This is not necessarily a problem with a fairly large bonsai, but frankly, it can be downright ugly on a smaller one. The only solution is to let the young shoots "run their course." Prune above the first pair of leaves, and if these really seem too big to you, wait until they mature, becoming thick and dark green. Suspend all use of fertilizers, then cut all

the petioles, or leafstalks. Now expose your tree to a little more sun than usual. There is no risk to the leaves since it doesn't have any. In a few days, the rest of the leafstalks will fall and the axillary (the lateral or secondary) buds will develop to give rise to new shoots. Water it copiously, then allow it to dry out a little more than usual. This process will wear out the tree, forcing it to make smaller leaves. A lot of work, but well rewarded.

This process of exhausting your tree should be undertaken only when absolutely necessary. Be advised that the *Acer palmatum* and *Acer buergerianum* or *trifidum* are the only ones that can withstand it, and then, only when they are adults and in great shape.

Common name: *Japanese maple*
Latin name: *Acer palmatum "Corticosa"*
Age: *40/45 years old*
Size: *20 in (50 cm)*
Shape: *Moyogi*
Outdoor
Origin: *Japan*
Collection: *Rémy Samson*

A Heart of Gold

The *Acer buergerianum* or *trifidum* is a favorite among the Japanese. Of the Japanese maples, it makes the smallest leaves, shaped rather like those of the ivy, and gilded in autumn. Its boughs are thin, delicate, and very well shaped and its trunk grows quickly. These very appealing qualities make it an extraordinary bonsai and thus quite popular.

A happy marriage

Thanks to its extreme adapability, the trident maple is very often used for the *Ishitsuki* shape. This is the style in which the bonsai's roots are trained to grow embracing a stone. The process begins by having the young tree grow very long roots in a deep pot containing a very sandy mixture. Then you attach the trunk and roots to the rock with raffia or aluminum wire covered with rubber so as not to scar the bark. The whole is then set in the pot and covered with soil and moss, even that part of the roots later destined to be visible. Young roots exposed to the open air would dry out and could not grow to grip the rock.

Distinguished by strength

This is a species that appreciates full sun except in the middle of summer, when you must provide it adequate shade. You must water it thoroughly and fertilize it well because this is a very vigorous plant. Consequently, it also requires constant pruning. Be vigilant: because the trident maple produces shoots that can leave impressions quickly, the trunk can be indelibly marked in a very short time. Ordinarily, only the first pair of leaves is kept. When the tree becomes older, even these must be nipped off. This is done with very long tweezers, and should be done almost monthly. This inhibits its growth and forces it to remain very compact. Repot the tree every three or four years. If it is trained in the *Ishitsuki* style, have the wisdom to protect the tree well in winter because its root system is very vulnerable. The roots are just below the surface so as to dramatize the rock. If its foliage is overlarge, treat it as you would the Japanese maple: induce total defoliation after the first flush of growth. Remember though that this is appropriate only for healthy adult foliage, to allow time for the buds to form.

So much to recommend it

The trident maple is as lovely on a rock as it is when cultivated in the formal upright shape or in the semi-cascade. This is because it is wired very easily in young or green wood. The wood becomes very brittle and easy to break as it matures, however, so wiring must be done early and quickly. Watch it carefully—sometimes barely two weeks is enough for a wire to damage your tree forever if it grows too tight.

Another advantage of this maple: it heals well and quickly, which allows it to suffer significant structural pruning without any evidence of it years later. A word of caution, though: be careful not to fertilize a tree which has just formed scars, because these too will grow, transforming into hideous blisters instead of fading into the bark.

Another attractive quality of this species is its capacity to make beautiful *Nebari*, or surface roots: as long as the tree grows, the roots that form the base will gradually link together. To assure a beautiful *Nebari* (a tree whose roots are a significant feature), take care not to release the tree too soon when you repot it. The Japanese often plant it with a carpet of peat moss to insulate the roots and encourage them to grow.

Common name: *Trident maple*
Latin Name: *Acer buergerianum*
Age: *35 years old*
Size: *18 in (45 cm)*
Shape: *Ishitsuki Outdoors*
Origin: *Japan*
Collection: *Rémy Samson*

The Ginkgo Tree

Common name:
Ginkgo tree
Latin name:
Ginkgo biloba
Age: *30 years old*
Size: *24 in (60 cm)*
Shape: *Chokkan*
Outdoors
Origin: *Japan*
Collection: *Rémy Samson*

In autumn, its leaves are gilded, from which it derives its common name in French: 24 carats (*40 écus*). It is a veritable splendor. Its gentle passage from dull green to golden yellow is prolonged, all the better to savor it. But its truest rapture is the tender green spring shoots that appear at the extremity of each twig. The *Ginkgo* is an extremely resistant tree—tradition holds that it was the only plant to survive the effects of the atomic bomb at Hiroshima. Its resistance to pollution is naturally presumed.

A loner

Generally, the *Ginkgo biloba* is treated as a solitary subject, reduced somewhat in height to make the trunk grow, and is almost without lateral branches. Its growth is very strong and not easily contained. Moreover, this deciduous conifer is not made of "wood" in the usual sense: its "branches" are very short and unusually thick, not woody at all, and almost impossible to wire. Since it is exceptionally difficult to shape, it is almost always worked in a way to emphasize the trunk covered with leaves, whence comes its massive, very majestic appearance.

A large bonsai rather than a small one

The *Ginkgo* is fairly easy to cultivate, it appreciates full sun, except of course, at the height of summer, and it likes a lot of water. Since it grows very quickly, you must give it solid fertilizer from the end of April to the end of October. Repot it every two or three years with a mixture fairly rich in compost or humus.

Pruning should be done with scissors in the spring. Allow the young shoots to "run their course" before cutting them above the second or third leaf. Because its small branches are so very thick and its leaves cannot be reduced to a size appropriate to a smaller specimen, the *Ginkgo* serves best as a medium or large bonsai.

Boy or girl

The *Ginkgo biloba* is a dioecious tree, that is, each tree has only one type of gamete—it is male or female. In order to obtain seeds, you must grow both male and female plants. This is a delicate matter because the pulp that surrounds the core of the seed emits the unpleasant smell of vomit towards the end of fall, making the females not so popular. The roasted seed, however, seems to be a delicacy.

Silvery White Reflections

Common name:
Japanese beech
Latin name: *Fagus crenata*
Age*: 20 years old*
Size*: 15 in (35 cm)*
Outdoor
Shape: *Chokkan*
Origin: *Japan*
Collection: *Rémy Samson*

A shimmering white solitary trunk planted solidly in its pot, boughs reaching skyward: the tree is impressive. In summer, the contrast is accentuated by very pretty, green, embossed, slightly lacy leaves. But it is in winter, when the beech tree is without leaves, that it is at the height of its beauty. Like all marcescent trees (which do not fully shed their leaves), it is capable of retaining its dry foliage until spring.

Fagus crenata is the variety that the Japanese use. Its foliage is crinkled and embossed, and its trunk is a more pure white than that of *Fagus sylvatica*, which is rather light gray and very smooth, but with the same silvery reflection.

It grows quickly

This tree develops and its trunk thickens rapidly. A few years are sufficient to produce a beautiful bonsai.

It appreciates fairly high humidity, and tolerates only indirect sunlight in the heat of summer. It must be watered regularly and abundantly or you risk drying out the edges of the leaves. A healthy eater, the beech requires monthly fertilizing from May to October.

The hardest cut...

Normally, the beech tree sends out a single shoot per year—a very long one with such tender, hairy, crumpled, deep pink, baby leaves that you will feel cruel to cut it. You must be strong. This is the only way to maintain its shape while forcing it to produce a second series of shoots somewhere around the end of May or the beginning of June. Keep only one leaf, or two at most, and only one on the crown.

Its rather brittle wood should be wired early, before the young shoots have matured. Should you wish to modify the shape of a large branch, use a very thick wire covered with paper and raffia. In any case, and as always, watch the tree's growth conscientiously to keep it from being marked.

Charm
and Elegance

Common name:
Chinese hackberry
Latin name: *Celtis sinensis*
Age: *50/60 years old*
Shape: *Chokkan*
Indoor/Outdoor
Origin: *Taiwan*
Collection: *Rémy Samson*

The Chinese hackberry is heralded as a beautiful deciduous tree with a silvery trunk, whose bark is smooth when it is young, and slightly cracked when it is older. Its pale green foliage suggests that of its cousin, the elm, though the *Celtis* has leaves more round and lacy.

This tree is often cultivated as a solitary subject in the *Moyogi*, or informal upright shape. Like the elm, it inspires a certain respect. It takes on a venerable appearance very young, and it is difficult to conceive of it in other, less formal, shapes.

Clarifying its origin

Its sensitivity to the cold is its Achilles' heel. Even if the Chinese hackberry resists it fairly well, the *Celtis australis*, cannot. On the other hand, it is entirely satisfied when it is hot in the winter. Consequently, it is classified as both an indoor and an outdoor species. Therefore, you must be clear about its origin, knowing that if it comes from the South of China or Taiwan, it will adapt very well as an indoor bonsai;

conversely, if it comes from Japan, it will risk dying of heat. Its shape can help to define its origin.

In South China, the *Celtis* are very large subjects taken from nature, then transformed into bonsai. They are grown in very large pots, often even placed in courtyards or gardens. In winter, they can withstand temperatures close to freezing, and in summer, high heat and humidity. Those from Japan are in general smaller and resemble model trees. They are deciduous and must live outside.

The conditions of cultivation for *Celtis*, whether the outdoor or indoor variety, are identical to those for elms. Even so, indoor specimens prefer temperatures a little lower, ideally 51 or 52°F (16 or 17°C), and a lot of light. This will allow them the period of rest that they enjoy in their natural habitat.

The *Stewartia monadelpha*

[A Confection of a Tree]

Common and Latin name: *Stewartia monadelpha*
Age: *40 years old*
Size: *22 in (55 cm)*
Shape: *Moyogi*
Outdoor
Origin: *Japan*
Collection: *Rémy Samson*

This tree bears a soft, sensual, dark orange bark so appealing to the touch, and even the taste, that you might call it decadent. It has small, tender green leaves with an endearing fuzziness, edged with a slightly darker border. This marvelous plant is from the *Camellia* family, and puts forth a similar very pure, simple white bloom. In every season, this tree is true enchantment: in the fall, there is its foliage; in the spring, its flowers; and in the winter....

A true classic

Alas, this little marvel is somewhat refined—it can be sensitive and easy to distress. Its delicate branches are especially intolerant of cold and icy wind. And this princess of a tree has a very particular need for water free of calcium. For all this, it offers considerable charm.

This tree is rarely imported—in fact it is little cultivated in Japan. It therefore represents the essence of collecting, the same as the Chinese hackberry. From time to time, a large importer will order young plants or bonsai, and this is the time for you to try it.

A delicate broad-leafed tree

Stewartia monadelpha does not like the burning sun of summer, so put it in the shade. Mist it regularly because a dry, hot wind can burn the edges of its tender leaves.

Ideally, it is entirely content to rest on a large plate with a layer of moist sand or gravel, a little like an indoor bonsai, only outside. Its pruning is the same as for all the broad-leafed trees: allow only two leaves for each shoot. Because its growth is not especially vigorous, it needs pruning no more than twice a year.

Its wood is very brittle, so be careful that the wiring does not mark it. *Stewartia monadelpha* must be repotted every two to four years when young, in an acidic

Water quality

Water quality is basic. Because the majority of plants treated as bonsai come from acidic or neutral soil, they suffer from being watered repeatedly with hard water. You will notice it leaves a white deposit along the edges of the tree's foliage and around the trunk and the edge of the pot. This problem does not exist in Japan where the city water is filtered free of calcium.

Elsewhere, bonsai lovers have found diverse solutions: they collect rainwater (even polluted rainwater from a large city is preferable), they shop in pet stores for aquarium buffs (who share a similar concern), or they buy bottles of distilled water. Intense consumption can get expensive.

mixture. Add a little peat moss to retain more water. Fertilize it from the time it gets its adult foliage until the end of October.

Sugar and Spice

Common name:
Cotoneaster
Latin name:
Cotoneaster hori-
zontalis
Age: *25/30 years*
old
Size: *16 in (40 cm)*
Shape: *Moyogi*
Outdoor
Origin: *France*
Collection: *Rémy*
Samson

Somewhat like *Pyracantha*, the *Cotoneaster horizontalis* has small semi-evergreen leaves; the *Cotoneaster salicifolius* has leaves more like the willow's. The foliage remains a brilliant green year round. The small, pink flowers give rise to red fruit of which blackbirds are particularly fond. If you can protect this fruit from birds, it will remain on the tree for a good portion of the winter. Sometimes the tree even bears its new bloom and the preceding year's fruit simultaneously.

Simple maintenance

The *Cotoneaster* is easy to cultivate. It prefers the sun, except of course at the height of summer. Water consistently and carefully because, like all fruit trees, it risks losing its fruit if it is thirsty for very long. Repot it every two years, and fertilize from the moment the fruit forms until October.

Resistant to shaping

The *Cotoneaster horizontalis* is a ground-hugging shrub with leaves arranged along its branches like bones along a fish's spine. To look its best, you should avoid giving it a very regular shape; a free form, like a bush, suits it very well, similar to the treatment recommended for the Japanese quince tree. It is utterly unsuitable for the formal upright shape.

Wiring it is a real trick because the wire must go between the leaves, which grow very close together. Watch carefully that the wire does not scar the branches: the fruit draws a lot of sap, which makes the trunk and branches grow quickly.

Prune it rigorously because it grows quickly in all directions.

Supple wood

The *Cotoneaster salicifolius* has a more classic bearing and lends itself better to the *Moyogi* and *Shakan* styles. Because its leaves are a little longer, a more vertical shape will show it off to advantage.

Its wood is very easy to work all year, but

significant shaping to "redesign" it should
be done in the spring to make the most of
its hardy growth. Its sweetly feminine
quality is nicely complemented by pots
rich in shape and color.

The Hornbeam

[Her Royal Majesty]

Common name:
Hornbeam
Latin name:
Carpinus coreana
Age: *20/25 years old*
Size: *12/15 in (30/35 cm)*
Shape: *Yose-ue*
Outdoor
Origin: *Japan*
Collection: *Rémy Samson*

Never more beautiful than when it is almost vertical, the hornbeam is massive, majestic, imposing, powerful. This is why it is most commonly trained to the *Moyogi* (informal upright) or *Shakan* (slanting) shape, giving it the venerable aspect of an old forest dweller.

The hornbeam has all the natural qualities of a beautiful bonsai. Not surprisingly, it is the Asian species that gives the best results. Favored by the Japanese and Chinese for centuries, they have the great advantage of naturally small leaves. A leaf already small requires so much less shrinking....

This tree is characterized by a slightly silvery, veined trunk that rapidly assumes the silhouette of a beautiful, knotty old tree, its branches twisting slightly under the weight of the ages. Its very fine and delicate boughs give it the appearance of an adult tree very early on.

Gone with the "wind"

The *Carpinus coreana* has reddish leafstalks and very small, fairly round leaves, half the size of those of the common hornbeam. The leaves of the Japanese *Carpinus laxiflora* are more pointed, a little like those of the *Carpinus betulus* here. Both wear shades of orange in the fall even more pronounced than the elm, and they tend to be marcescent, that is, they keep their dry leaves for part of the winter. If you choose to "supplement the wind" by gently removing these leaves, do so before the budding begins to avoid damaging the buds.

The hornbeam can tolerate some sun, but like all broad-leafed trees, it must avoid the burning rays of midday, so keep it out of the sun between noon and 4:00P.M. At the same time, be aware that, if it is too often in the shade, its internodes will lengthen and it will lose its lovely autumn color.

Fertilize it particularly in the fall. This thickens its trunk. It should be repotted

every three or four years, before the
appearance of its first leaves.

As with elms, unglazed pots in deeper
shades show off the beauty of this tree.

Red Berries, Silver Trunk

Ilex serrata and *Ilex sieboldii* have long been favorites with florists. Their large, silvery-gray branches covered with small, very brilliant red berries are ubiquitous in winter. You may not know that this is actually the fruit of the female holly.

The Japanese dote on the holly. Its silvery-gray trunk is a marvel in itself. It supports thin delicate branches ornamented with foliage that is first violet in the spring, then tender green; the backs of the leaves and the leafstalks remain slightly purplish. The naturally small, fairly straight, sharp-edged leaves are easy to shrink.

The better half

Ilex serrata is dioecious (specimens are either male or female). Around the end of April and beginning of May, the female stem produces flowers. When fertilized, they will give rise in the fall to small round vivid red berries. Only the female *Ilex* is cultivated as a bonsai, and it is very common in Japan. The male is not used because it does not bear fruit. If you want the pleasure of the holly's berries, however, you must plant a male somewhere nearby. Sometimes, growers mix female and male plants in miniature forests or bouquets of holly, which promotes pollination. With or without fruit, the tree is a nice addition to your collection.

Sun-loving

The majority of the time, this tree is cultivated as an isolated subject with a thick massive, trunk. But its very thin boughs permit the arranging of bouquets of a particularly great delicacy as well.

Easy to cultivate, it tolerates sun very well, except in the hottest hours of summer. Moreover, unlike many other broad-leafed trees, it needs the sun to flower and to give it its autumn colors. It can stand some dryness between watering, except when it bears fruit; the least forgetfulness will end in their falling off.

Despite its apparent frailty, it is not especially susceptible to cold, though it is advisable to protect it from icy wind and extremely low temperatures.

In view of its very rapid growth, the holly demands very careful and abundant feeding, particularly if it is young or producing fruit. Wait for the berries to begin to form a bit before giving it solid fertilizer.

Cut it back

The holly needs to be pruned severely and very regularly because its powerful shoots, despite their seeming refinement, have been known to make a branch grow quickly out of proportion to the tree. It is ideal to keep only the second and third leaves at the time of the first growth, then a single one during successive growth periods. If you do not grow any male subjects, prune them severely all the same because flower buds form only on the current year's growth. Eliminate the buds that often appear at the base of the trunk, for they will take all the sap to the detriment of the crown. The Japanese exploit this tendency to produce buds at the base to obtain a large trunk. They plant the tree in the ground and leave it there for four or five years. Every year they cut it back, that is, they prune the branches and the head in order to force the trunk, which grows almost to resemble a bulb. At the end of this period, the tree is uprooted, severely pruned again, then filled with putty to mask the scars. When the small buds on the trunk give rise to branches of 4 or 6 inches (10 or 15 centimeters), these will be shaped; because the holly has a brittle wood, only the tender branches are worked.

Common name: *Deciduous holly*
Latin name: *Ilex serrata*
Age: *25 years old*
Size: *10.5 in (26 cm)*
Shape: *Yose-ue*
Outdoors
Origin: *Japan*
Collection: *Bruno Delmer*

The Birch

[Silver Bark]

Common name:
Birch
Latin name: *Betula verrucosa*
Age: *20/25 years old*
Size: *18 in (45 cm)*
Shape: *Moyogi*
Outdoor
Origin: *France*
Collection: *Rémy Samson*

The birch is a beautiful, gracious tree with thin and delicate boughs. Its most distinctive and appealing feature is its silver-white bark, which strangely resembles paper. Its fresh green leaves are very small and shaped like lacy hearts, and turn a golden color in autumn. Cultivated as a bonsai, these qualities are unchanged.

A "star" seldom seen

You would think this tree's resistance to cold, disease, and neglect would make it a star. The fact is that it is so common that it is rarely chosen for bonsai collections. The exotic species are more attractive than a tree that grows on every street corner. It also has the unattractive tendency to branch out slightly and to make fairly long internodes, so it is adaptable only as a fairly large bonsai (from 16 to 20 inches, 40 to 50 centimeters).

Avoid following its natural growth habit, which would be the straight broom style, and treat it rather in a slightly tortuous shape, *Moyogi* or *Shakan*. It will gain in beauty and value, and you will gain experience. Despite its strong resistance, spare it any burning summer exposure and mist it in the evening. It appreciates regular watering but be mindful not to let it dry too much, or its foliage will suffer.

Unwilling to make small leaves

Repot it every two or three years in a mixture containing enough compost to retain water.

Glazed pots in daring shades of blue or green will show off its beautiful bark.

Since it is not inclined to make small leaves, give it fertilizer only around mid-July until the end of October. Prune it normally, but remember that its wood does not grow very quickly and that it is fairly brittle, so is easily scarred by wiring. Be willing to scrounge around nurseries; you might be lucky enough to find a birch naturally somewhat contorted that would be a perfect candidate for a bonsai.

[A Mediterranean Native]

Common name:
Cork oak
Latin name:
Quercus suber
Age: *18/20 years old*
Size: *24 in (60 cm)*
Shape: *Formal upright*
Outdoor
Origin: *France*
Collection: *Rémy Samson*

All the beauty of the *Quercus suber*, or cork oak, resides in its simplicity and its natural appearance. It has a deeply cracked, stocky trunk with a gray bark and small, matte green leaves edged with sharp teeth. This slightly curved evergreen with a very Mediterranean appearance is a standout in the *Moyogi* shape, especially in a rather sober pot. It likes full sun, and can tolerate wind and rain, but not in excess. It generally grows in dryer, hotter regions and does not enjoy a cold winter. Its magnificent cousin, the evergreen oak (*Quercus ilex*), has a beautiful, deeply scored gray bark and also prefers a winter sheltered from the icy wind. However, with adequate shelter and if its soil is not too wet, it can resist fairly low temperatures.

Propitious qualities

These trees are rarely treated as bonsai. They are familiar chiefly to the inhabitants of Southern Europe; they are mostly collectors' plants in Asia, where the summer is too humid for them. Be that as it may, these oaks, compared to their European cousins, the red oak and pin oak, can give very good results, because their boughs are thin and their internodes short, both qualities essential to beautiful bonsai.

As with all broad-leafed evergreens, repot them every three or four years in a mixture fairly poor in humus. Water them thoroughly and let them dry. Fertilize them once their foliage has become mature, towards the end of July (the oak has only one flush of growth).

Pruning for the cork oak is like that of an ordinary broad-leafed tree. Keep one or two leaves. Be very careful though: this species tends to scar. The best course is to begin the tree as a young plant and hide the wound of a sacrifice branch with another branch.

Evergreen Trees

Bee Pleaser

Common name:
Burning bush
Latin name:
Pyracantha angustifolia
Age: *40 years old*
Size: *22 in (55 cm)*
Shape: *Ishitsuki*
Outdoor
Origin: *Japan*
Collection: *Rémy Samson*

The *Pyracantha angustifolia* is sometimes known as the burning bush. It grows virtually everywhere. It has fairly small, dark semi-evergreen foliage, pretty and abundant white blossoms and, depending on the variety, small fruit of yellow, red, or orange. Its only drawback, and a painful one: its plentiful sharp thorns.

Its fragrant white blossoms alone—in April and May—merit its cultivation; they certainly draw the admiration of the bees. Cultivation as a bonsai actually enables a greater appreciation for this plant than is possible when planted full-size in the ground. The thorns grow smaller too!

Do it yourself

Little cultivated in Japan, the *Pyracantha angustifolia* as a bonsai is not found very often here either. Therefore, you must make it yourself. The bush is very common though, so it is fairly easy to procure at very affordable prices. As in nature, slightly worked shapes, such as *Moyogi* or *Shakan*, suit it well. A more vertical posture is difficult to imagine for it: it never occurs thus in nature. A bonsai is always more beautiful when it seems natural.

As with all flowering and fruit bearing trees, reducing its foliage size is not easy. Accordingly, it is better to limit the size of the tree to 16 to 20 inches (40 to 50 centimeters); the berries will be more proportional then.

A tree without problems

It should be repotted every two years before the first flush of growth, towards the end of February or the beginning of March. Serious pruning for shape is done in winter when the tree has lost some of its foliage. If necessary, you can help the shedding process along. Maintenance pruning on the young shoots is done in summer, before the wood has matured. The *Pyracantha* prefers full sun, but a prolonged thirst puts the fruit at risk.

As with all fruit trees, monthly feeding with solid fertilizer is imperative from May to October, except during its bloom, when an excess of fertilizer can abort it. Its most formidable enemy is the aphid, which sucks its sap. The honeydew produced by the aphids settles on the leaves, and a black mold (fumagine) can develop on it. As with all bonsai, careful regular inspection will prevent or minimize this problem.

The Yew

Noble and Austere

Common name:
Yew
Latin name: *Taxus baccata*
Age: *50/55 years old*
Size: *15 in (35 cm)*
Shape: *Chokkan*
Outdoor
Origin: *France*
Collection: *Rémy Samson*

Try to catch it blanketed in snow…the sight is a real eye-pleaser. Here is a tree that rarely occupies the place that it deserves—it is too often confined to a landscaping role as hedge or topiary. This beautiful conifer develops small, slightly shiny, dark green needles that contrast strongly with its rugged bark, usually a red-brown. It sports pretty red, somewhat translucent berries; we hardly notice them in the gray of December, yet they are the happiness of birds. But be forewarned: this plant is toxic!

A theatricality of rigor

The Japanese almost always train the yew as a formal upright with the trunk partly stripped, as if lightning has hit the top and torn off a strip of bark, and some branches that have turned white by the action of wind and rain. A real production, this—

and it actually enhances the evergreen foliage. The tree's serious appearance seems to unleash the most unbridled fantasies. At the same time, it lends itself to a minimum of rigor and theatricality. Cultivate it in an extremely sober pot, which will heighten its severe beauty.

It takes its time

Taxus baccata (or *Taxus cuspidata*) grows easily. Although in the garden the species has a fairly slow growth rate, it has ideal rhythm in a pot. The spring shoots are not very long and pruning them by two-thirds with a shears is all you do.

Wiring should be done in winter before the buds open. The needles growing so close together is the greatest challenge here, a little like the *Juniperus rigida:* passing the wire between the needles without damaging them or the branch you are training is difficult. If you do not succeed, they will immediately turn yellow. Otherwise, because the growth of the tree is not very rapid, you can leave a wire in

place for nearly a year. Fertilize it only from June to October, and repot a young tree every two or three years, every three or four years when it is older. Avoid very hot exposures, and let it spend the summer in the shade. The yew prefers some humidity, so mist it regularly, particularly in the evening. Let it dry a little between watering, but just a little.

The Strength of Eternity

A small pine tree in a blue pot—the classic image of a bonsai. Along with the Japanese maple, the Japanese white, or five-needle, pine is the tree that most evokes the Empire of the Rising Sun. Traditionally, as the symbol of longevity, this tree is a favorite of the Japanese. It lives to be old—very old—representing at once the power and the strength of eternity. It knows that it has time.

A venerable appearance

Wiring its needled branches in plateaus gives the tree a venerable appearance very early. Its bluish gray-green needles, growing in small tufts, stand out against a silvery smooth bark when it is young. The bark cracks and thickens with age, giving a fairly accurate idea of the tree's real age. If to this you add a certain "malleability" unique to conifers, it is clear why this tree has become a "star" of bonsai. No collection is complete without it.

Sun above all

Easy to live with, the Japanese white pine needs only to be cultivated outside in full sunlight. It handily endures the wind, rain and cold. It cannot grow indoors. In fact, the success of its cultivation depends on its time in the sun. Without the sun, the needles and the tender shoots will lengthen unattractively. At the height of summer, of course, it requires some shelter; left in the full sun for long, it will cook. Should this occur, water it, put it in the shade and wait for the tree to form small new buds as the burnt needles fall.

Understand its needs

The only really tricky thing is watering because *Pinus pentaphylla* (also known as *Pinus parviflora*), like *Pinus thunbergii*, needs a certain lack of water to keep its needles small. In nature, this tree develops at high altitudes and in rocky crevasses, where rain reaches it with difficulty. As a grower, you must reproduce these conditions in the pot. Shoots not watered enough remain too small and can even be aborted. Overwatering will cause the needles to grow long, and since their cycle of renewal is three years, they will be around a long time. Little by little, you will learn the limits of the tree and you will know when to water it.

Pine trees must be fed very carefully, starting in the middle of July, when the needles have reached their adult size. Then, apply solid fertilizer monthly until the end of October. A good application of fertilizer in autumn will encourage the thickening of the trunk. Repot young subjects every three or four years on average, and every six or seven years when older. Be mindful that the roots of pine trees live in symbiosis with a fungus that causes a whitish felting between the pot and the roots; its delicious mushroom odor, most apparent when repotting, is a sign of your bonsai's good health.

Prune to shape

Shape pruning can proceed only when the needles are fully mature, so take advantage of winter and do it then. Every year, the tufts of needles grow a little longer, and even if you leave only one third of the spring growth on the crown and two-thirds for the shoots on the lower branches, the bonsai will continue to grow. Every two or three years, redo the foliage plateaus.

Some bonsai lovers worry about discovering tiny violet "pine cones" that appear in the spring, just under the new shoots. These are in fact sacs of pollen which will soon dry out and fall. They are really rather pretty; the only down side is that the pollen makes the shoots grow longer.

Common name: *Japanese white pine* **Latin name:** *Pinus pentaphylla* **Age:** *70 years old* **Size:** *36 in (90 cm)* **Shape:** *Fukinagashi* **Outdoor** **Origin:** *Japan* **Collection:** *Hideo Kato*

Virile

This species is virile, par excellence: the powerful, straight, magnificent tree, even "sitting" in its pot, reaches impressively for the sky. The cracked bark, the somber trunk: they are a gripping contrast to the bright green needles, so healthy and fresh. The Japanese black pine (*Pinus thunbergii*) greatly resembles the European black pine (*Pinus nigra*), except that the latter has darker needles, as the name indicates. One might say that the Japanese black is the "male" counterpart of the Japanese white pine (*Pinus pentaphylla* or *parviflora*).

Eternal trees

Very popular but cultivated mostly in the hot and humid south of the Japanese archipelago, this pine tree lends itself to almost all bonsai shapes. Its size ranges from 6 inches to over 36 (15 centimeters to over 90). The tree's life span is very long, and the imperial collection at Tokyo possesses some subjects that may be at least 450 years old. In a sense, the eternal bonsai....

This species is hardly ever seen in Europe because its importation has been prohibited for years for reasons of sanitation. The subjects now found there were imported long ago. It is too bad because this is an easy species for bonsai. It is grown commercially in the U.S. for bonsai and as a common landscaping tree.

With foliage to match

The Japanese place considerable value on a tree's *Nebari* (surface roots). They cut the plantlet to assure attractive *Nebari*, then they allow the trunk to grow.

Next—and here rests the difficulty—it is important for your bonsai pine to have foliage in proportion to its size. You must force it to make small needles. The trick is to keep the tree thirsty without killing it, once the "candles" (or shoots) are pinched back two-thirds.

Pruning to shape the pine tree is done in winter, at the latest before the beginning of spring. Use very solid copper ties because

they harden with time and take on a discreet gray-green color. Because the branches and trunk thicken slowly, you can leave them in place from one year to 18 months, checking them from time to time.

Very old subjects are to be repotted every five or six years, young ones, every three or four years, in a soil or mix without humus or compost. Like the Japanese white pine, the black pine's roots live in symbiosis with a fungus that makes felt around the pot, a sign that the tree is in excellent health.

The Essence of Romanticism

Common name:
Juniper
Latin name:
Juniperus rigida
Age: *20/25 years old*
Size: *36 in (90 cm)*
Shape: *Chokkan*
Outdoor
Origin: *Japan*
Collection: *Rémy Samson*

Jagged, bleached, crackled, torn, and loaded with dead branches, the trunk reaches for the sky.... *Juniperus rigida* lends itself particularly well to a dramatic presentation. It is the vision of a tree high in the mountains, prey to the fury of the elements: the howling wind, the biting cold, and the rocks that hurtle down. In reality, this very solid species normally grows fairly straight in a compact form.

A lover of humidity

From a rather rapid growth, this tree develops a fairly thick trunk with red-brown bark. Its green-blue foliage, edged with white, is made of small, very pointy needles. Although in nature it grows in fairly arid climates, as a bonsai it appreciates humidity. The cold and snow will give its foliage a pretty, slightly rusty color, which will disappear in the spring. This very solid species likes the open air, the sun, wind, rain, and snow, but cannot bear the burning summer sun. Because *Juniperus rigida* can tolerate no excessive dryness, be sure to mist it morning and evening and to place it on a plate over a layer of moist sand or gravel in the summer.

With its very powerful root system, the juniper must be copiously fed with solid fertilizer each month from April to the end of October.

Good for every shape

The juniper is easy to treat as a bonsai because its branches, even when old, can generate new buds and thus repair themselves. This is a quality valuable to bonsai enthusiasts. And its ready response to wiring means that it lends itself to almost every shape, a little like the pine tree. This is an opportunity to give free rein to your craziest imaginings without fear of being ridiculous. Keep in mind though, that the more wild the shape of the bonsai, the more conservative the pot should be. Stick with simple clay and pure lines to underline the tree's beauty.

Maintenance pruning is very simple. All you have to do is hold the base of the new needle tuft with one hand, and with the other, draw on its extremity in order to clip at least two-thirds of the shoot, without breaking the edges of the needles that you want to keep. This process should be repeated as it grows, which means nearly all summer. The more you do it, the more new buds your tree will send out, giving it a fuller, more beautiful shape. Conversely, if you let the young shoots "run their course," this will hollow out the interior. Older subjects must be repotted every four or five years, younger ones every two or three years.

This juniper, about 100 years old, originated in Japan, and measures 32 inches (80 centimeters). It belongs to the collection of Rémy Samson.

[The Essence of Femininity]

As the *Juniperus rigida* is masculine, virile, thorny, and rigid (as its name attests), so is the *Juniperus chinensis* feminine, soft, supple, and round. Even in the most extraordinary shapes, the Chinese juniper is never hard—dramatic, certainly—but always voluptuous.

Its very compact dark green foliage resembles a succession of small tiles with tender green, almost yellow, shoots displayed against an almost red trunk. In Japan, to highlight the coloration of the bark, any part that begins to turn gray is very gently removed. In China, on the other hand, they prefer to leave this gray bark untouched; for the most part, it is eventually exfoliated.

The tree takes shape

The Chinese shape the juniper bonsai almost as a ball in order to show off its multiple trunks. Those in the Land of the Rising Sun far prefer to use the capacity of this species to survive extreme conditions by torturing it into very exceptional shapes. Just as with the *Juniperus rigida*, they endeavor to achieve drama. With *Juniperus chinensis*, it is the tree's serpentine flexibility that is magnified.

The horticulturist who models Chinese juniper bonsai starts from the rough trunk, as nature has made it, around which he shapes the foliage and the lateral branches. The plants are first grown in an open field so that they may grow wider and taller very quickly. Fixed on bamboo stakes, their trunks will grow somewhat twisted. A few years later, they will be dug up and carefully put in plastic nursery pots. Another two or three years and these simple nursery subjects will become bonsai, under the ministrations of professional hands.

The trees thus obtained will be sold a few years later, repotted in pretty ceramic planters with the foliage nicely pruned in a plateau shape.

In a hot and humid climate, this process is fairly rapid: between five and 15 years,

Common name:
Chinese juniper
Latin name:
Juniperus chinensis (sargentii)
Age: *50/60 years old*
Size: *32 in (80 cm)*
Shape: *Natural*
Outdoor
Origin: *China*
Collection: *Rémy Samson*

Common name:
Chinese juniper
Latin name:
*Juniperus chinensis
(sargentii)*
Age: *35 years old*
Size: *20 in (50 cm)*
Shape: *Shakan*
Outdoor
Origin: *Japan*
Collection: *Rémy
Samson*

depending on the desired size. In other climates, it can take much longer. In response, savvy bonsai lovers have learned to search for "treasures" in nursery "bargain bins," which overflow with sickly and twisted plants of all types.

Yearning to breathe free

The Chinese juniper is not very demanding, except on the issue of atmospheric humidity. Be sure to mist it regularly and set it over a plate with water or moist sand or gravel. It loves the sun, except, of course, in the hottest hours of summer. Since it is originally from hot and humid climes, remember to water it regularly in the evenings, especially in the summer. Wind, rain, and the open air are its joy in life, as for all outdoor bonsai. The cold and snow make its foliage turn brown, but only temporarily.

It grows quickly and, like all gourmands, demands a regular supply of solid fertilizer from the beginning of May to the end of October.

Although it has overlapping scales, rather than needles, it is pruned in the same manner as its cousin, the *Juniperus rigida*.

A Miraculous Bloom

Common name:
Azalea
Latin name:
Rhododendron indicum
Age: *30 years old*
Size: *9 in (22 cm)*
Shape: *Moyogi*
Outdoor
Origin: *Japan*
Collection:
Japanese

This azalea is about 10 years old, a native of Japan, and measures 18 inches (45 centimeters). It belongs to the collection of Rémy Samson (photo page 95).

The mass of flowers is so overwhelming that it drowns the foliage. In every color and every shape, azaleas meet with a success even greater that of the quince tree—which inspired a big enough craze itself. The Japanese are so fond of the azalea that they are continually creating new varieties; exhibits spring up nearly everywhere to celebrate each one. And why not? This fabulous bloom on a smooth, knotty, dark ochre trunk is a pretty unforgettable spectacle.

It needs acidity

The azalea needs heat and humidity to renew its foliage after it blooms, but an equally great need is that for slightly acidic water. This plant, which grows in heath soil, also needs an acidic compost. Add a little peat and compost of decomposed leaves to the normal soil mixture.

Cultivate it in the shade when the temperature becomes too high, above 68 to 70°F (20 to 22°C). Mist it and watch the watering because the plant can "dry out" only in July and August, the period when its buds will transform into either flowers…or leaves.

In case of excess watering—if the month of August is very humid, for example—you risk not having spring flowers. Repot it each year after its bloom, and give it a lot of fertilizer from three weeks after it is repotted until the end of June.

The azalea must also undergo severe pruning after its bloom. Cut all of its small branches very short because the plant flowers only on the wood from the previous year. If you fail to do this, it will double in volume in one year. Thus, in Japan, it is not rare to see an almost bare trunk with the beginnings of buds or the spreading out of its branches.

The Exquisite Orange

Common name:
Mock orange
Latin name:
Fortunella hinsii
Age: *25 years old*
Size: *24 in (60 cm)*
Shape: *Moyogi*
Indoor/Outdoor
Origin: *Japan*
Collection: *Rémy Samson*

How can one resist such charm: a small dark green foliage, a smooth trunk evoking the skin of a serpent, proffering the smallest of what nature can create in an orange: a true jewel—hardly larger than a cherry, barely smaller than a kumquat. In Japan, this is cultivated more in the South. In the region of Tokyo, it is put in an unheated greenhouse, out of the ice in the winter.

Mixed maintenance

In more northern regions, it must be treated simultaneously as an indoor bonsai in winter, offering it warmth, and an outdoor bonsai in summer, when the temperature rises above 50 to 54ºF (10 to 12ºC) at night. Do not hesitate to put it in full sunlight, but avoid the hottest hours of summer.

Proper cultivation encourages small, narrow foliage and a good bloom at the end of spring. Do not prune it too short because the tree blooms on the most recent shoots. Wait for the fruit formation to be complete in order to reduce its growth, and proceed with pruning in the autumn, once the fruit has fallen.

The *Fortunella hinsii* must be repotted every year, in the spring, in a fertile mixture that drains fairly well. Add a little sand and leaf compost if necessary. Its roots rot easily, so avoid excess moisture—let it dry a little between watering.

The very brittle wood is difficult to wire because it breaks so easily. The simplest solution is to let it dry a little beforehand because, when the tree is thirsty, its green wood is more supple. Avoid having to wire an old branch; it will break. Be careful, the tree is quickly marked because of its rapid growth.

The rather delicate appearance of this orange tree makes it a special favorite of miniature bonsai lovers. Similarly delicate pots in bright colors and complex shapes make magnificent containers for it.

The Boxwood

[A Test of Patience]

Here is a plant very well suited to treatment as a bonsai. A big part of its appeal is its brilliant foliage of a fairly dark green. The leaves are small and evergreen. In the spring, the tender young shoots are a verdant explosion. The trunk of the boxwood tree is a smooth yellow ochre (for the outdoor species) and grows very slowly, making its training as a bonsai long and difficult.

The majority of boxwood bonsai come from trees collected in the mountains or in forests (*Yama-dori*), a practice now prohibited except by agreement with the landowner. Unfortunately, this is the only means for quickly obtaining a boxwood tree of the right size. This aside, you can always try searching for one in the "bowels" of a nursery; with a little luck, you may get your hands on an interesting plant already possessing a trunk of just the right size. Its small, compact foliage and its restrained growth encourage growers to keep the boxwood in a miniature bonsai shape, or at least a small bonsai, of no more than 16 inches (40 centimeters).

Give me a little of your time

The hectic rhythm of life today threatens to corrupt the bonsai enthusiast: once the watering is done, the shade put in place, he may have the serenity of one who has finished his work. What a mistake! At least once a week, depending on the size of your collection, and every week without fail, you must consecrate two or three minutes to each tree. This is not much, but it demands sitting down and carefully assessing your trees, one by one. This important routine permits you to uncover parasites, adjust the wires that begin to mark the trunk or branches, or simply foresee the need for modifications or work down the line.

Easy to maintain

Whether the *sempervirens* or *angustifolia* (or Kingsville), the boxwood thrives equally in full sunlight or shade. As always, at the height of summer, leave it in the shade to avoid its ultimate "cooking." At the same time, watch its watering because, while the tree resists a relative dryness, a mistake can cause the appearance of necrosis on the young leaves.

Since it grows very slowly, repotting it every three or four years while it is young (every five years, once the tree is an adult), is sufficient. A good, classic mixture with a little more humus suits it perfectly. Be sure to feed it well in order to compensate for the relative infrequency of repotting.

Hard to shape

This very hardy tree adapts to the most diverse shapes. It is adaptable as well to the cascade as to the formal upright shape, without looking silly in either. The difficulty—and a significant one—is that it must be shaped when the wood is very green and tender. Barely mature, the wood becomes astonishingly brittle. On the other hand, the boxwood readily sends out buds, even on the old wood, which explains why even an old tree may be easily transformed into a bonsai.

Buxus harlandii, originating in tropical or subtropical regions, can live indoors fairly well. With a nicely cracked trunk and very narrow leaves, it is happy simply placed in front of a window, in a fairly warm room. A high degree of atmospheric humidity is best.

Common name: *Chinese boxwood*
Latin name: *Buxus harlandii*
Age: *20/25 years old*
Size: *15 in (35 cm)*
Shape: *Broom style*
Indoor
Origin: *China*
Collection: *Rémy Samson*

The Sacred Bamboo

[Grace and Lightness]

Common name:
Sacred bamboo
Latin name:
Nandina domestica
Age: *24 years old*
Size: *5.5 in (14 cm)*
Shape: *Natural*
Outdoor
Origin: *Japan*
Collection: *Bruno Delmer*

"Bamboo of heaven." This is what the Chinese call this bush, and it is more a bush than a tree. It seems to grow reluctantly, and its fairly cracked gray-black trunk thickens very slowly. Its incredible foliage—bright green, very jagged, extremely thin, delicate, and horizontal—is decorated in the most amazing colors throughout the year. An excess of sun, and it goes completely red. A slight cold front and it turns purple. When spring comes, it turns yellow orange with very bright green shoots. It loses few of its leaves and seems rather ethereal—an eminently gracious and gentle plant.

It asks for very little

In the ground, *Nandina domestica* puts out long clusters of small white flowers that last a long time and it has a very brilliant fruit, intensely red, which lasts all winter. But as a bonsai in a pot, it is fairly rare to see it bloom and bear fruit. The beauty of its foliage, in fact, is pleasure enough.

The majority of bamboo bonsai sold commercially are of Chinese origin; the Japanese prefer them as garden specimens. The *Nandina domestica* is happy in a more moist soil mix. And full sunlight favors its pretty colors, even at the height of summer. Allow it to dry between watering, even severely, and feed it only from the end of August to September. Because it grows very slowly, *Nandina domestica* does not actually require shaping. In fact, its wood is not wired; the tree is restrained instead—forced to remain a miniature bush, rather than worked. Undoubtedly, it is for this reason that the Japanese discount its many good qualities.

It is repotted every four or five years. The roots, which have a tendency eventually to make the plant grow up out of its pot, are a deep yellow and give off a very strong scent when they are cut.

The Ivy

[Disarmingly Modest]

If you look past its humble appearance, the ivy is a treasure. The evergreen creeper grows everywhere in anonymity, but shows a certain style at the first cold spell, its foliage decked out in dark red and green marbled with white. A slight attack of frost accentuates this even more without making you lament the plant.

The "Glory of Marengo" variety, with its tiny leaves veined with yellow ochre, sends out a touch of cheerfulness and color from the depths of winter until spring, when the young, deep yellow shoots push through the soil.

So much to love about it

The essential climber, the ivy (*Hedera helix*) bonsai is made particularly beautiful by a slanting shape, such as *Shakan*, cascade or semi-cascade. Remember, the art of bonsai is that of magnifying the natural bearing of the plant. The naturally somber foliage will benefit by being displayed in a pot of intense color or exceptional shape.

The ivy is extremely resistant: dryness, shade, full sun, even weed killer (almost!), nothing harms it—it resists! Scale is its only real threat.

Despite its numerous attractive qualities, it remains rare as a bonsai. The plant grows like a weed everywhere, as you have surely noticed, so it is easy to find mature ivy which can quickly make a beautiful bonsai. Its foliage is easy to shrink, and its growth is vigorous. Once the plant has its definitive shape, at the end of spring, cut all the leaves to the level of the leafstalk. Expose the ivy to full sunlight, and in a few days, you will see the leafstalks turn yellow, then fall, allowing numerous small buds to pierce through. Above all, do not feed it at this time, but water abundantly. Reduce the watering significantly at the appearance of the first leaf, so as to force the plant to make very small leaves. Prune it above the first or second leaf and the ivy will branch out better. Repeat this process on average every two years to refresh the foliage.

Light sensitive

In normal conditions (except for the multi-colored varieties), full sunlight is very suitable to the ivy, even in the summer. Let it dry fairly well between watering in order to control its growth and maintain its miniature leaves. Apply fertilizer in August and September, as with the pines. This makes the trunk grow and has little influence on foliage size.

Repot it every three or four years—more often when it is young, because it needs to build up its foundation structure.

Prune it often, before shoots reach three or four leaves, unless you want to make the trunk or a branch grow. Otherwise your tree may grow hollow in the center by losing inner leaves.

This is a highly photo-reactive plant; its leaves turn very quickly towards a light source. It is vital to rotate it regularly before the light so that its growth remains symmetrical.

Common name:
Ivy
Latin name:
Hedera helix
Age: *25 years old*
Size: *20 in (50 cm)*
Shape: *Shakan*
Outdoor
Origin: *France*
Collection: *Rémy Samson*

A Delicate Creeper

This delicate creeper is utter rapture! The delicate, shiny, semi-evergreen foliage takes on a delightful diversity of colors throughout the year. In the course of the seasons, the brilliant leaves, with a base color of beautiful medium green, will be marbled with red, yellow, orange, and rust. The coloration of this plant is always interesting; it never has two identical leaves. Autumn hosts its best display, of course. The leaves, by then predominantly red, flutter off at the slightest breeze; they will be strewn across your bonsai shelf, where they will take their time turning brown.

Cousins

The *Trachelospermum asiaticum* grows very quickly, producing long, very thin stems bearing facing leaves every inch or inch and a half (two or three centimeters). In the garden, this plant is fairly invasive, which may explain why it is cultivated less often than its cousin, *Trachelospermum jasminoides*. The variety *Jasminoides* makes divinely fragrant flowers of which

the Italians are so fond that they plant it everywhere—in pots, on terraces, and in gardens. In May, the cities are all fragrant with it. And since this plant thrives with virtually no care, it is found truly everywhere.

Cultivated as a bonsai, the species does not flower, but it produces pleasingly decorative foliage. Moreover, *Trachelospermum jasminoides* is superbly adaptable to training as a bonsai. The species as bonsai is seldom seen in Japan, as it is not native there. The only tricky part with this tree is to make it grow a thick trunk rapidly. A technique developed by the Japanese for this purpose is simply to braid together several stems which, in rooting and thickening, will fuse to form a trunk. Each stem will then engender one branch. At the end of several years, it is absolutely impossible to discern what technique has been used!

Just as it is best to make a fairly large bonsai of the *Trachelospemum jasminoides* (from 16 to 20 inches, 40 to 50 centimeters) because of its leaf size, so must the *Trachelospemum asiaticum* be treated as a miniature bonsai or *Kusa-mono*.

No problem

These two species do not enjoy very harsh cold. Shelter them from wind and low temperatures in winter. Apart from this, both these plants are worry-free. They are resistant to the sun, which only accents their beautiful colors, they tolerate dryness (they originate in the Mediterranean), they are easily pruned, they can be wired with no problem, and they grow rather quickly.

To maintain a beautiful shape, prune the *Trachelospermum* regularly and fairly severely. Like all creepers, it needs to be well fed, and should be repotted every two or three years because its root system is invasive.

Despite its appeal, *Trachelospermum asiaticum* is very rarely found. Imported only seldom and equally little known, it has much to gain by leaving the "ghetto" of the plant collection.

Common name:
Asian Jasmine
Latin name:
Trachelospermum asiaticum
Age: *15 years old*
Size: *11 in (28 cm)*
Shape: *Natural*
Outdoor
Origin: *Japan*
Collection: *Rémy Samson*

[Classic Elegance]

Common name:
Japanese cedar
Latin name:
Cryptomeria japonica
Age: *45 years old*
Size: *36 in (90 cm)*
Shape: *Chokkan*
Outdoor
Origin: *Japan*
Collection: *Rémy Samson*

This Japanese species is typically found in the formal upright style. Its powerful and slender trunk, whose very soft bark flakes off, has branches sufficiently bare to magnify its aged appearance. The foliage, which somewhat resembles that of the juniper, is very soft and of a magnificent, tender green that the first cold spell sometimes turns a deep shade of rust.

It appreciates a humid atmosphere

This very beautiful tree is found only where there is adequate humidity. Native to hot and humid regions, it prefers a dry winter but is able to withstand the cold. Its need for humid summers and dry winters make it little treated as a bonsai.

Place it on a plate on a layer of moist sand or gravel in the summer, in light shade, and mist it generously in the morning and evening. The rest of the year, you can leave it outside in the garden or on a balcony.

It likes water, and you should avoid letting it dry too much between watering. But be careful to use only rain water, not hard water, because it prefers acidic soil. Keeping this in mind, supplement its soil mixture with a little peat moss and leaf compost. To prune the *Cryptomeria japonica*, pinch shoots back two-thirds. Hold the shoot between the index finger and thumb of one hand and pull on it sharply with the other to detach two-thirds.

Wiring to reshape the tree is done on average every two years. Fertilize from the end of June until October.

It's All in the Foliage

Common name: *False cypress, Hinoki cypress*
Latin name: *Chamaecyparis obtusa*
Age: *35/40 years old*
Size: *18 in (45 cm)*
Shape: *Chokkan*
Outdoor
Origin: *Japan*
Collection: *Rémy Samson*

This congenial conifer is very common in gardens, perhaps a bit less so as a bonsai. Its growth is compact and fairly quick. Its foliage is flat and evergreen, and shaped rather like a spoon. Its dark green color may turn reddish brown with the first frost, and becomes a tender green in the spring. Its young shoots are almost yellow. Its trunk can grow very thick with age, and its dark red bark tends to come off in strips. The "Nana" variety—the joy of rock or dwarf conifer lovers—is especially well known. Bonsai enthusiasts prefer the standard species, a tree whose bearing is truly majestic.

Pruning is required

The false cypress has a fairly rapid growth, which obliges you to prune it at least two or three times a season, like the Chinese juniper. Avoid burning exposure to full sun; it prefers, on the contrary, some atmospheric humidity.

Put it in the shade in midsummer, and leave it outside the rest of the year. Be careful not to let it dry out too much between watering, but don't soak it either; as with all conifers, an excess of water can cause serious decay. Its soil mixture must be adjusted accordingly: put a little more humus or compost to retain the water.

The false cypress is easy to shape: keep only the useful branches, and remember the rule of three points when wiring its branches. Its foliage will turn by itself to put itself in the right position.

Apply solid fertilizer only from July to October in order to avoid excessive growth. Watch out for spider mites, its chief predator. Treat it immediately if the foliage becomes lead gray or yellow.

Repot the *Chamaecyparis* every three or four years. Choose a conservative pot in unglazed clay to show its beautiful foliage to advantage.

Deep Freezer

Common name: *Ezo Spruce*
Latin name: *Picea jezoensis*
Age: *25/30 years old*
Size: *36 in (90 cm)*
Shape: *Formal upright*
Outdoor
Origin: *Japan*
Collection: *Rémy Samson*

The Japanese vow a great love for the *Picea jezoensis*. It is the tree, par excellence, of *Hokkaido*, the northernmost island of Japan, where the winter is long, cold, and rigorous. Professionals have always made expeditions there to search for these hardy spruces trained by hostile nature into bonsai. Their needles are minuscule and very dark green, and their trunks are twisted by the wind. Too bad the importation of these magnificent trees has long been prohibited to the U.S. and Europe for fear of disease. But planting cuttings of this species works very well.

It goes for humidity and coolness

If you cannot provide it coolness and humidity, forget it. The spruce demands shade (facing east) and humidity and hates atmospheric dryness and pollution. It is satisfied with nothing less than sitting on a moist layer of sand or gravel in the shade.

Given these conditions, it is extremely hardy; it is often planted on rocks. Unlike in the atmosphere, it resists dryness in the soil very well (but not as much as the *Pinus pentaphylla*); its efficient use of ambient humidity allows it to remain dry for a long while. You must mist it regularly however.

The spruce is easily pruned, like the *Juniperus rigida*: pull off two-thirds length of the spring shoots with your fingers. Its wood is not easily marked because it does not grow quickly. The more you prune it, the more you push its branches to "fill out" with foliage. Fertilize it from July to October, and repot it every four or five years in a mixture with a little compost.

In general, its beautiful black bark and dark green foliage are complemented by unglazed, earth tone pots in somewhat restrained designs.

The Pomegranate

[A Sublime Trunk]

Common name:
Pomegranate
Latin name:
Punica granatum
Age: *20 years old*
Size: *15 in (35 cm)*
Shape: *Moyogi*
Outdoor
Origin: *China*
Collection: *Rémy Samson*

A walk through the Luxembourg gardens or the Orangerie de Versailles is enough to make one understand why this tree arouses such passion. The trunk twists, cracks, furrows, and channels fairly early for a bonsai. Very soft when it is young, the tree's bark takes on the appearance of cracked yellow ochre mountains or sand.

Its fairly narrow, bright green foliage tipped with red has the perfect dimensions. And its bloom is a great joy: large bright red buds giving way to beautiful intense red flowers. Grown as a bonsai, the tree produces fruit charmingly small but with rapid growth, although professionals for some years have been perfecting miniature varieties.

Neither too hot nor too cold

So why do we not encounter this jewel more often? Very simply because its preferred habitat is a Mediterranean garden. North of Tokyo, the Japanese keep it in an unheated greenhouse during winter. In Osaka, as in China or Taiwan farther South, it remains outdoors. Indoors, it is often too hot, unless it is placed against a large, cool picture window. Outdoors, it is often too cold. Ideally, it should be treated it as a deciduous bonsai outdoors, well protected in the winter. Expose it to full sunlight, water it thoroughly, and fertilize it from May to October.

Prune the young shoots only once it has begun blooming or you might cut the immature floral buds too early. Its blooming period begins fairly late because the *Punica granatum* needs to be very hot. So it bears fruit fairly late, too. The pomegranate season peaks at the end of autumn.

Like all fruit trees, repot it at least every two years (yearly if it bears fruit) in a mixture fairly rich in compost.

Don't be afraid to use pots in outrageous shapes and colors; this tree only gains from being displayed in a container as strong as it is.

Wood like glass

Shaping it is simple. The pomegranate heals fairly well after pruning. But its wood is like glass; it must be shaped very early while it is still somewhat malleable. Work only on green wood, being careful to cover the wire with raffia or paper to prevent marks.

The older the wood is, the more arduous this task becomes. For this reason, very fine old subjects are rather rare and, generally, they are Japanese. The Chinese produce nice specimens, but they are young.

Tropical Trees

The Tree of a Thousand Stars

Common Name:
Snow rose or Serissa
Latin name: *Serissa foetida*
Age: *55/60 years old*
Size: *28 in (70 cm)*
Shape: *Moyogi*
Indoor
Origin: *China*
Collection: *Rémy Samson*

This small bush has delicate dark green leaves and is covered with tiny white trumpets at the end of spring and in the summer. As a very pretty indoor bonsai, it can flower fairly regularly during the winter.

Its many assets provide for a beautiful bonsai: pretty leaves, delicate flowers, rather fine light ochre branches, and a trunk that is naturally somewhat twisted. Its only drawback may be the fetid odor put out by its roots when they are cut. On the whole, the tree is really easy to live with.

A little thirst makes it supple

The *Serissa foetida* is a subtropical plant. It can live very well outside as long as it is protected from freezing. In Japan, the plant lives outside all year, except in the North. Indoors, place your tree as close as possible to a window, in a room that is not too hot. Always keep in mind that the hotter it is, the more the tree needs light and moisture.

Thanks to its vigorous growth, *Serissa foetida* produces results quickly, so it needs to be pruned often. Be careful not to cut the buds, though. You must also take care to cut off shoots at the base and on the trunk, unless you plan to make cuttings from them. Shaping is done by severe pruning after it blooms or at the end of the spring so as to allow it to renew itself.

Wiring is not very easy because, like so many trees, it has very brittle wood. Therefore, you must shape either the mature wood—that which has become yellow ochre—or the young green branches, after inducing mild thirst. When it is about to "go into a nose dive," it becomes much more supple: this is the time to go to work. You can water it after it is pruned. If you feel it has suffered unduly from the drying out, you can water the bonsai thoroughly and then leave it in a clear plastic bag for a few hours. Remember to feed it regularly from March to October with solid bonsai fertilizer.

A relative bargain

Since it is easy to make cuttings, you can
even start one from scratch. But a medium
size bonsai is generally so reasonably
priced, why deny yourself the immediate
gratification? If you choose to buy one,
repot it in the spring with at least one-
third traditional soil in a base of compost
and humus, which will reduce the risks of
careless watering. The *Serissa* does not
like to dry out. Always keep its soil moist,
but not soaking. The tree is normally
repotted in the spring, on average every
two or three years.

The Orange Jasmine

An Intoxicating Fragrance

Common name:
Orange jasmine
Latin name:
Murraya paniculata
Age: *35 years old*
Size: *18 in (45 cm)*
Shape: *Formal upright*
Indoor
Origin: *Taiwan*
Collection: *Mr. Phung*

They say in Taiwan that an orange jasmine in bloom can be smelled from more than 3.5 miles (6 kilometers) away. The fragrance is very strong indeed. The flower clusters themselves, however, are small and discreet. This bush is worth the trouble of its cultivation if only for its bloom. The jagged green foliage shines almost as if it were polished and the soft smooth trunk, warm ochre in color, entices the touch.

Its range is vast

The orange jasmine is a subtropical plant whose habitat is vast. It is not picky: it enjoys cultivation outdoors and where necessary, in unheated greenhouses.

Indoors, it is ideal to place the *Murraya paniculata* in front of a well-lit window, facing east or west in winter. Keep it in a room that is not overheated, resting on a plate with a layer of moist sand or gravel. Spending summer—when it blooms—on the terrace or balcony, or in the garden, will fill in its leafless gaps. Acclimate it to the sun gradually to encourage the appearance of floral buds. One day you will notice an exquisitely intoxicating fragrance: your orange jasmine is in bloom! With a little luck, you will soon have the pleasure of its small red fruit.

A rather large bonsai

Its foliage has an appearance that is better adapted to rather large trees. The majority of *Murraya paniculata* available on the market are from China. After having been taken from nature, they have been shaped into bonsai. It is only very recently that it became possible to find attractive trees of a smaller size, around 20 or 24 inches (50 or 60 centimeters), which are better suited to a smaller space.

It flowers on the current year's wood, so cut or prune it only after it has bloomed. It is fairly easy to wire the green wood, but the wood becomes brittle once it is matured and very difficult to work. While it must never really dry out between watering, the tree cannot stand continually being very wet either. So be vigilant.

Once the bloom has passed, apply solid fertilizer as long as it remains outside. If the climate does not permit you to take it outside, use fertilizer for "flowering plants," diluted as indicated.

Its worst enemy is the aphid and low humidity in winter makes it prey to spider mites.

The Ficus

[Lasting Happiness]

Common name:
Ficus
Latin name: *Ficus retusa*
Age: *20/30 years old*
Size: *12 in (30 cm)*
Shape: *Moyogi, Neagari*
Indoor
Origin: *Taiwan*
Collection: *Bruno Delmer*
Photo page 120

Age: *20/22 years old*
Size: *8.5 in (21 cm)*
Shape: *Moyogi*
Indoor
Origin: *France*
Collection: *Bruno Delmer*
Photo page 121

A magnificent knotty trunk whose exposed roots cascade towards earth to wrap the globe in their tentacle-like arms and branches heavy with leaves reaching toward the ground: this is the lord of the tropical forest, at least among bonsai.

The *Ficus* is very impressive in nature, and so it is as a bonsai. Whether it is 10 or 36 inches (25 or 90 centimeters), whether miniature or very large, it remains the best adapted and the most beautiful indoor bonsai. It lives in very diverse latitudes from Monte Carlo to Taiwan because it can tolerate a wide range of temperatures. It can even withstand a light freeze if its soil is dry. The tree is ideal for a first acquaintance with the art of bonsai. And the easiest variety in this species is the *Ficus retusa*, whose pointed brilliant green leaves are naturally small and solid. It branches out very willingly and puts out buds with no problem, even on an old trunk or an aged branch.

The tree for all conditions
Put it in front of a well-lit window, exposed to the east in summer and the west in winter, and turn it regularly so that all sides receive equal light. Whatever the season or the light source, this will assure symmetrical development.

Common name: *Ficus*
Latin name: *Ficus retusa*
Age: *45/50 years old*
Size: *3 ft (1.10 m)*
Shape: *Triple Neagari*
Indoor
Origin: *Taiwan*
Collection: *Mr. Phung*
*Photos pages 122 and 123
(bottom)*

Though the tree is not especially sensitive to temperature, avoid exposing it to drafts or to sudden changes in temperature all the same, as with all indoor plants.

Watering is a crucial point because this tree's trunk is saturated with water, like that of the baobab. It is imperative that the tree be allowed to get very dry between watering. To water it, place the bonsai in a basin deep enough so that the water level rises to the top of the pot. Leave it like this for five or six minutes, enough time for the soil to be well saturated, then let it drain for about 10 minutes before putting the bonsai back on the shelf. As long as the soil does not become very light (i.e., powdery) and does not detach from the edge of the pot, you should not proceed with another watering; this corresponds to approximately one or two days without water in summer, and around one week in winter. This depends as well on the volume of soil to foliage. It is important to feed the *Ficus* well because its growth is vigorous. In the summer, as for all indoor bonsai, remember to apply solid fertilizer outside because of its rather strong odor. Limit the use of liquid fertilizer to two or three times per month in the summer, in order to compensate for the eventual lack of solid fertilizer, and dilute it at least three times more than is indicated. Suspend all fertilizer during the period of foliage renewal.

It must renew its leaves

The *Ficus* is the only indoor bonsai for which it may be necessary to make it renew its leaves, just like an outdoor bonsai. After a winter spent indoors, its leaves grow a little "soft" and often too large. In mid-June, in this case, you should cut them all to the level of the leafstalk, then prune the edges of the buds. It will very rapidly be covered with small tender new buds. Actually, it is unfortunate that few *Ficus* are subjected to this treatment because there is nothing more beautiful than a *Ficus* with leaves completely in proportion to its size. In Taiwan, where the most beautiful *Ficus* bonsai are found, this treatment is performed twice a year. A side benefit is that it enables collectors to judge the quality of the *Ficus* and the work done to cultivate it.

In general, this defoliation is accompanied by good shape pruning, eliminating branches that are too fat, and wiring to modify the shape. Be careful because the *Ficus* grows very quickly; watch that the branches are not marked.

Maintenance pruning is very simple. Keep one leaf on average per shoot.

Repot the tree regularly, every three or four years when it is young or in formation, and every five or six years after that. Be sure to mix a third or a quarter of the original soil in the new soil mixture to aid in its revival—this advice is valid for all indoor bonsai. The *Ficus* must never be watered just after repotting. Wait three or four days—the time that it takes the cuts made to the root system to close up. Mist during this period two to three times a day to prevent the tree from being thirsty.

The tree is subject to attack by aphids and spider mites. Check it regularly in order to find and treat the problem in time. Treat as indicated on product label and repeat a few days later. Avoid all misting during the treatment.

Common name: *Willow leaved fig*
Latin name: *Ficus nerifolia*
Age: *15 years old*
Size: *10 in (25 cm)*
Shape: *Broom style*
Indoor
Origin: *Taiwan*
Collection: *Rémy Samson*

[Large and Lanky]

**Common and
Latin name:**
*Podocarpus macro-
phyllus var. maki*
Age: *40 years old*
Size: *3ft (1.10 m)*
Shape: *Moyogi*
Indoor
Origin: *China*
Collection: *Mr.
Phung*

A shaggy, very deep green conifer without a single really typical shape, this unkempt-looking tree draws attention for its lanky bearing and spiky foliage. The branches are not bare like those of the pine: they bristle with large flat waxy needles gathered in shiny clumps. From time to time, they turn yellow and fall. The trunk is covered with a thin bark that tends to peel off a bit.

This very resistant Asian native tolerates cold well, allowing it to live outside in more temperate regions and, farther north, to spend winters sheltered on a covered porch or in a cold greenhouse.

Never as it is in nature

The Chinese generally grow this tree in the garden, very closely pruned, with the foliage removed or shaped into fat balls or plateaus (as they prefer in Japan). It seems to invite the most stylized shaping; as a bonsai, it is not often shaped as it is in nature. On the other hand, it is fair to assume that *Podocarpus* accepts training for shape with few problems.

It is most often treated as a fairly large bonsai, having good-sized foliage, but cultivators in populist China also make smaller ones that are quite attractive. In Japan, it remains a garden species. It is not traditionally cultivated there as a bonsai.

It needs a lot of light

Its need for light is significant: keep it in front of a window and turn it regularly. Artificial lighting is another alternative; it can keep the tree from losing too many needles in winter. Be sure to let the *Podocarpus maki* dry a little between watering because its roots do not tolerate excessive moisture. Fertilize it only once its needles have developed; they can otherwise grow very long. Even more than thirst, adequate intense light will force it to grow small proportionate needles. Nevertheless, be careful not to give it too much sun.

The tropical bonsai of China

The territory covered by China and Taiwan is vast and so has an unusually wide range of climatic conditions. With a long tradition of bonsai cultivation, this country exports species that will adapt to greater or lesser degrees depending on the places of their origination. Among the trees that originate in a hot and humid tropical climate are the Ficus, Carmona, Chinese Elm *and* Sageretia. *All these trees acclimate well to life indoors at temperatures between 64 and 68°F (18 and 20°C) when placed on a moist plate in front of a window. Those trees from relatively cooler tropical climates, such as the* Murraya, Serissa, Podocarpus, *and pomegranate, prefer temperatures from around 57 to 64°F (14 to 16° to18°C) maximum.*

Repot it every four or five years in a mixture that is not too fertile and give it a fairly large, deep pot so as to help it withstand some dryness between watering.

Mist it regularly. It prefers to pass the summer outdoors in very light shade. Maintenance pruning is the same as that for the *Pinus pentaphylla*: keep only a third of the shoot, but prune it with scissors because its wood is fairly hard.

The Fukien Tea Tree

[Fruit and Flowers]

Common name:
Fukien tea tree
Latin name:
Carmona microphylla
Age: *20/25 years old*
Size: *12 in (30 cm)*
Shape: *Moyogi*
Indoor
Origin: *China*
Collection: *Rémy Samson*

Bearing small, fuzzy, deep green leaves on a smooth beige trunk and making tiny white flowers that give way to pretty little orange berries, the *Carmona* has all the prerequisites to tempt the bonsai lover. It thrives indoors and is very forgiving of your mistakes. Should you move it at an inconvenient time or put it directly in an air current, it will lose the majority of its leaves. But in a few days, it will start to remake them as quickly as it lost them. And if you neglect to water it, a certain wilting will occur; water it thoroughly, as you would the tropical Chinese elm, and a few hours later it will regain its allure.

It adapts well

Originating in subtropical Southeast Asia, *Carmona* adapts to a wide range of indoor environments, even fairly warm ones. But it really hates sudden changes of temperature or humidity. Keep it on a layer of expanded clay marbles kept moist, or on some moist sand. Place it where it will get from 12 to 14 hours of light per day, either natural or artificial, from November to February. This will enable it to keep its leaves in winter. A lack of light for indoor bonsai is almost always evidenced as a significant loss of leaves.

A little moisture and fertilizer

It grows quickly and its internodes are short, so it keeps its shape with little effort. Its rapid growth also allows it to be shaped fairly quickly. Be sure to avoid its drying out too much between watering as this can severely damage young roots. If you are unsure, it is better for the soil to be a little too moist than not moist enough.

From May to October, give it only solid fertilizer; the liquid form can be too rapidly absorbed, causing burns to the root system. Feeding the bonsai outside in the summer, in a shady spot, will dispel the

fertilizer's unpleasant odor. But remember to bring the bonsai in when the night temperatures begin to fall as it eases into autumn.

Be careful, spider mites are fond of this tree and they can cause considerable damage. Be prompt to treat the problem with an appropriate pesticide.

The *Carmona* has wood that is not particularly supple, but it is easy to wire and shape when still green, so it makes a compliant bonsai. You can easily find appropriate young specimens at reasonable prices, and the tree is easily propagatable from cuttings. Old subjects almost always come from *Yama-dori*, and their beauty testifies to the care they have received.

The Sageretia Theezans

As Fine as Silk

Common and Latin name:
Sageretia theezans
Age: *70/100 years old*
Size: *32 in (80 cm)*
Shape: *Free Moyogi*
Indoor
Origin: *China*
Collection: *Rémy Samson*

Its foliage resembles tender green silk, its boughs are of an extraordinary thinness, and its often massive trunk has somber bark that peels off in sheets like that of the sycamore. It is certainly one of the finest and most delicate species to live indoors. It prefers temperatures that are not too high in winter, like those in South China or Taiwan, the regions of its origin. As with all indoor bonsai, you must offset higher temperatures with increased humidity.

Taken from nature

The majority of *Sageretia theezans* come from *Yama-dori*, taken from nature and made into bonsai. Put in the ground for a while to recuperate, then potted and sculpted, they can be sold as bonsai in somewhere between two and five years.

This tree grows fairly quickly, but the delicacy of its boughs demonstrates that the branches and trunk have a very slow growth rhythm. Propagation from cuttings is not a real option, as the leaves have a tendency to rot in any appreciable humidity. Your best bet is to buy the most interesting and attractive specimen you can find. But be careful, the wood is very brittle, and any wiring at all is nearly impossible. In fact, this bonsai is most truly Chinese in the sense that its shape is achieved almost entirely by pruning.

Limit the "shock" of repotting

Repotting a bonsai imported from Chinese is very tricky because of the very dense clay used there as potting mix. The tree must be repotted every two or three years when young, and every four to six when mature. In the process of repotting, it is vital to keep at least one third of the original soil. Reduce it into powder as fine as possible before incorporating it into the new soil mix, always at the rate of at least a third. This will lessen the trauma of repotting, at the same time fostering the tree's recovery in the new mixture.

keep it outside in full shade. The least bit of sun will cook its leaves and branches. Even without direct sun, its vigorous growth requires frequent pruning to keep its shape and produce new buds.

Adequate light in winter, whether natural or artificial, will keep it from losing its leaves. Adequate in this case means 12 to 14 hours a day from November to the end of February.

Delicacy above all

The extreme delicacy of its foliage allows you to anticipate its needs. First, avoid drafts and extreme temperature changes. Keep the *Sageretia theezans* in a cool and humid atmosphere, with a layer of moist sand or gravel under it.

Its soil should never dry completely or be soaking wet. Remember to mist the tops and undersides of its leaves. In summer,

[Leopard-Skin Bark]

Common and Latin name: *Eugenia cauliflora*
Age: *25/30 years old*
Size: *18 in (45 cm)*
Shape: *Moyogi*
Indoor
Origin: *Indonesia*
Collection: *Rémy Samson*

Eugenia cauliflora—commonly called "Cherry of Cayenne"—is a beautiful tropical species originating in Indonesia. Its cousin, *Eugenia uniflora*, hails from Guyana. Its smooth bark resembles leopard skin: it has a light ochre base marked with distinctive brown spots. The tree has very thin boughs that accentuate its sprawling attitude and its very tender green foliage is pleasingly petite. It produces a delicious fruit.

It lives well indoors

Eugenia cauliflora's white bloom is ravishing—it grows on stalks in clusters. Indoors, it prefers full sunlight, in front of a window facing east, if possible. Keep some moisture under it, say some damp sand or clay on a plate, and watch that the temperature is not too high. In the summer, give it full shade. Mist it regularly. Never let the soil dry completely because the rather delicate leaves will suffer, but also watch that the soil is not continually soaked. Fertilize it from April to September, and repot it only every three or four years. Prune it leaving one or two pairs of leaves, but only after the appearance of the buds. Be careful with wiring: the very fine boughs of the Eugenia are correspondingly brittle. On the other hand, the trunk grows very slowly and has less chance of being marked. Pots in rich colors will coordinate with its magnificent bark.

Kusa-
mono

The Kusa-mono

[Grass to Go]

Don't think that the Japanese limit their tinkering with nature only to the trees. They experiment as well with ferns and irises and grass, to the greater delight of bonsai lovers.

Called *Kusa-mono* (literally "grass objects" and, by extension "grass in a pot"), these are herbaceous plants, (i.e., having neither a trunk nor branches). This suggests a clump of prairie planted in a pot in all its airy lightness.

Some patience

The principle of *Kusa-mono* is the same as that of bonsai: miniaturization. A plant, of whatever kind, tends to reduce in size when grown in a very small container. But an herbaceous plant does not shrink as readily as a tree. A plant that produces wood is easily enough pruned to force the growth of shorter internodes and smaller foliage.

Herbaceous plants cannot be pruned. The conditions of cultivation alone force them to shrink themselves. Hence, the main feature of *Kusa-mono*: patience. Don't worry, it doesn't take as long as you might think. That

is because, ideally, you start with plants that are already fairly small. Shrunk further in pots, they become bonsai.

Kusa-mono is an integral part of bonsai presentation in your home. Bonsai nurseries and importers often grow and sell them these days, but since only fairly recently. *Kusa-mono* is a temptation tough to resist and bonsai lovers are already half-converted—the tiny decorative pot nestles the little plant so cozily—and the item is a bargain. In fact, what you are really paying for is the pot. The price can vary considerably for identical plants.

Growing a *Kusa-mono*

Choose a plant already fairly small and, if possible, an evergreen. At the beginning of spring, remove all the leaves that are too large. Take your future *Kusa-mono* out of its original cultivation pot and eliminate as much soil as possible. Cut back the superfluous roots and prepare the pot. Place a grill or a shard of pottery over the drainage hole to keep the soil from washing out and fix the grill to the pot with aluminum wire. Put a little soil mixture in

Bruno Delmer Collection

The pots

The untrained eye cannot easily distinguish between a valuable pot and one that is merely interesting. It may find a real treasure to be of no interest and be totally engaged by one that is very colorful, or that has a unique shape, but is without value.

In bonsai, certain pots are works of art in themselves; their price is linked to their design, the quality of their clay, the country of their origin, and of course, their age. A considerable part of a bonsai's value lies in pairing the tree with an appropriate pot, one that shares its origin. Whence come their escalating values....

the bottom, install the plant and pack it gently with a bamboo stick to repot it in the purest bonsai tradition.

Very rapidly, new, smaller leaves will appear and it will reach the ideal size: on average a quarter of its normal size, sometimes even less. A spot in full sunlight and some dryness between watering are conditions that encourage the foliage of most plants to shrink.

Use only solid fertilizer, after the blooming period if possible, from July to October. The recommended soil mixture is a little different from that for bonsai. It has a much finer particle size, relating to the size of the container. These minute pots can dry out very quickly. If you do not want your

passion to become a terrible slavery, add elements that retain water, such as peat, if your plant is acid-loving. Finely chopped sphagnum moss also retains water and will satisfy ferns, *Scirpus* (rush), and other humidity lovers.

Repotting should be regular and frequent. This occasion provides the opportunity to divide the plants and trade them with your friends. Repot at the very beginning of spring to nurture new roots. Remember to put your *Kusa-mono* in the shade occasionally or in a plastic bag or airtight box. In time, your little marvels may be ready to face a day in the open air.

The few examples that follow are applicable to most of the plants you might

Ophiopogon japonicus,
Bruno Delmer Collection

consider as candidates for *Kusa-mono*. Keep in mind that not all plants will look their best in miniature.

The Iris

The iris—small and charming—is perhaps the most popular *Kusa-mono* in Japan. They can be cultivated in pots ranging from the very large to those not much bigger than a thimble. The iris prefers humidity and cannot tolerate full sunlight in the summer. If the soil becomes too dry and the plants wilt a bit and start to yellow, plunge them into tepid water for a few minutes. Then drain them and set them in an airtight box overnight to recover. You can deter this annoyance by adding a little chopped sphagnum to their potting mix.

Generally, the higher the plant grows in the pot, the more attractive it will be. But at the end of two or three years, the rhizomes will force you to reduce the clump and divide them while repotting. Mist the irises regularly, especially in the evening. To reduce the rate of evaporation, arrange them on a plate full of moist sand. Do the

Outdoor iris, 20 years old, small size (barely 1.5 inches, 4 centimeters), Bruno Delmer Collection

same with the *Scirpus* (rush) or any plant more native to marshy regions. Add fertilizer only in July and August so as to limit growth.

In winter, their pretty tender green color can change to a dull yellow-green, similar to that they take on when they are thirsty. A fairly resistant species, they are content to wait for summer in a simple shelter. Just be sure they do not lack water.

The *Bergenia*

Here is a very pretty, hardy plant with beautiful large round leaves that are rather tough. Of an intense matte green, the foliage takes on vivid dark red autumnal colors. This plant's truest joy comes when winter weather starts: the terminal bud grows and a small floral shaft appears. The two or two and a half inch (five or six centimeter) bud will give at least a dozen pink flowers in winter. The frost accentuates the leaves' red winter coloration.

This very popular plant is reputed to be "tireless." Put it in dry, stony places in the shade or in full sunlight—in brief, almost anywhere. Buy a young *Bergenia* plant, or take a cutting from a flowerbed. Separate its rather tuberous roots and repot it in a clay- and sand-based mixture because the plant prefers to have dry roots.

More sunlight will force *Bergenia* to make only miniature leaves. It resists drought well, which also favors its pretty bloom.

Cut the dry leaves regularly. Fertilize it only in August, and repot it every two or three years.

Ferns

All species with little spores can produce ravishing hotpots. All you need to do is repot them in a mixture of clay and leaf compost. After watering, place your ferns in an airtight mini-greenhouse. In time, their very thin and fragile roots will colonize the new territory. Cultivate them in light shade in the summer, water them copiously and avoid drying wind. Just as for the *Bergenia*, a little fertilizer in August is plenty.

Repotting is optional; the charm of these hotpots is in the lushness of the plants' growth. In the end, it can even conceal the pot.

The rhizome (a rootlike stem that sends out both roots and shoots) is long and thin and carries almost circular tender, green spore-like bulbils. The rhizomes have a waxy appearance since they are fatty plants. Their propagation is easy, as outlined above: just take one or two bulbils fixed to a piece of

rhizome and place it in a mixture of clay and compost. A few months later, it will produce a new frond, which should be cared for gently before being put outdoors.

Japanese thrush

Characterized by discreet leaves in a very dark green ribbon, the Japanese thrush (*Ophiopogon japonicus*) has the good taste to make lovely purple flowers and to bear fruit. One very interesting variety that the Japanese use a lot in gardens has almost black foliage. It is a favorite because it grows quickly, colonizes small spaces, and remains low. It is propagated from root cuttings. One tuft can double in volume in one year. Its thick white roots force the plant up out of its pot so you will have to repot it every year. Prune the roots severely, keeping only a quarter of an inch (five or six millimeters) at most, before repotting in pure clay, if possible in May. You can cultivate the *Ophiopogon japonicus* in sun or shade. It can stand drying out between watering and should be given solid fertilizer in July and September. It also lives very well indoors. The Japanese thrush may allow you to add a *Kusa-mono* to your tropical bonsai collection. This plant has surely provided the avenue for a number of amateurs to discover the passion of *Kusa-mono*.

This list is far from exhaustive. Any plant with the requisite qualities, whether tropical or temperate, can be made a *Kusa-mono*. Why not try one?

Various outdoor ferns, 16 years old, 2 or 2.5 inches (5 or 6 centimeters), Bruno Delmer Collection

Bergenia saxifraga in bloom, 15 years old, 3.25 inches (8 centimeters), Bruno Delmer Collection

Keys to Success

1. Opening yourself up to the art of bonsai

The portraits of bonsai introduced you to the major characteristics of the most common species. Questions that might follow are, how do you buy a bonsai, or how do you make a bonsai? The most important thing is to differentiate between trees that live outside all year and those that live inside, to understand their different needs. Some lose their leaves in winter and others make fruit and so will need more fertile soil. Some must dry out between watering and others not at all. Before you decide to take the jump, know that bonsai, more than any other plant, require a lot of love and a certain instinct when it comes to gardening, a green thumb.

2. Buying the base soil

In Japan, certain nurseries keep the composition of their mixture secret. Others buy a ready-made all-purpose soil; they call it *Akadama-tsuchi*, meaning "soil from Akadama." Diverse mixtures are sold in garden centers, but Akadama soil is recommended. It is an almost red, nearly dry clay available in various-sized plastic sacks. Sift it according to your desired consistency. Clean, slightly acidic, it is perfectly suited to the majority of plants from Asia. One of its really great qualities is that during repotting it keeps its particle size even when wet, which allows the roots to clear a path very gently.
Plus, this clay disintegrates progressively to form a normally compact soil. Its price is fairly modest in Japan, and reasonably higher here because of the cost of transporting it. But it would really be bad to deprive your bonsai of such a base, which is especially suited to indoor bonsai.

3. Giving an indoor bonsai a good soil mix

Your tree's watering needs will not much affect the quality of the soil mix. For a tropical or subtropical bonsai, retain a quarter of the original soil during repotting. Once this is dried and crushed sufficiently fine to be used again, add it to your new soil.
For an indoor tree, potting mix should retain water, but not for too long, nor should it dry out too quickly. Supplement the gray clay popular in China sufficiently to nourish the tree and to assure that it not shrink up as it dries. Go for the following composition: 40% Japanese red clay (Akadama); 30% fine horticultural compost; at least 20% clay or soil from the tree's origin; and 10% sifted, fairly sandy soil (disinfected) from a vegetable garden. Refine the mixture according to the specific needs of each species. For example, for a *Ficus*, which must be very dry between watering, increase the *Akadama-tsuchi* portion at the expense of the horticultural compost. Conversely, for a *Serissa* or a *Carmona*, which prefer not to be too dry, use 40% compost and remove the vegetable garden soil.

4. Giving an outdoor bonsai a good soil mix

For outdoor bonsai, the principles are the same. But it is important to differentiate its needs

more particularly. Evergreens, like pines and yews, should be drier. For them, therefore, use 80% Japanese clay, 10% very fine compost, and a handful of vegetable garden soil. Please note: always be sure to sift the mix to eliminate debris such as small rocks, and use only the particle size appropriate to the size of the pot (very fine for miniature bonsai, a little larger leaves every year and they drink a lot. Consequently, the proportion of compost increases at the expense of the clay: 50% clay, 40% compost and 10% vegetable garden soil. This mixture is also sufficiently fertile to satisfy the large gourmands, like fruit trees, which are repotted every year.

If you have a large collection, or if you are a never look right, just as a beautiful watercolor in a bad frame loses its charm.

There is no end to the variety of pots available. Your choice is far more than a mere matter of taste. To choose, you must also know the secret of balancing a tree in a pot.

Imagine a scale: on one side, you have the volume of the foliage and, on the other, the mass of larger and more numerous the drainage holes must be. When repotting, fix a screen over these drainage holes to keep the soil from washing out. Ideally, the bottom of the pot should be concave, which prevents the water from standing there. It is up to you to be aware of this because pot designers sometimes forget it. Traditionally, conifers are potted in containers of unglazed

for a bonsai of 36 inches (90 centimeters). Plants such as the juniper, which do not like to dry out too much, prefer a base mixture of 70% clay, 20% compost, and 10% vegetable garden soil. A good practice is to disinfect your barely moist vegetable garden soil by putting it in a plastic bag and zapping it in the microwave. The broad-leafed trees need a soil much more rich in compost. They should re-grow their passionate and organized enthusiast, it can be very practical to have airtight containers with a ready-made mixture. Sometimes a terrible storm can snatch away the trees' soil, forcing you to repot them with all urgency and out of season.

5. Choosing the right pot
The pot is to the bonsai what a frame is to a painting. A beautiful tree in an average pot will soil. If you arrive at a balance, it is because your pot has the right volume. This analogy is a good point of departure. Then consider the thickness of the trunk, which should be equivalent, in the case of an adult tree, to the depth of the pot. As a very young tree is not worthy—before five or six years of age—to be put in a valuable pot, a terra cotta container is fine. Most important is that the pot drain well, and the larger it is, the rough clay, which allows the soil to dry more quickly. On the other hand, glazed pots, which reserve moisture, are best for broad-leafed trees. Even so, one sometimes sees conifers in China in glazed pots. This is more a question of taste because terra cotta can offer a greater variety of shapes, qualities, and subtle colors. Strictly speaking, there are no rules concerning color. Just try to keep in mind that the frame

must not be more admired than the painting; know how to choose a pot that is neither too striking nor too colorful. The art of bonsai is the art of balance.

The shapes of pots flow naturally as a function of the trees' shapes. Thick, square pots are generally reserved for "windswept" or "semi-cascade" styles.

Containers that are very high or very deep are

and fertilizer. It can no longer keep any in reserve.

In theory, the tree should have roots in the soil equivalent to its boughs. In fact, the main roots serve as its pivot, its anchor in the soil. The main roots bear the secondary roots and the rootlets, which grow non-stop. It is the latter which supply it with water and nutrition. The tree does not need

harsh conditions with few established roots and without an insulating layer of moss on the soil.

The process is therefore best done in the spring before the tree leafs out. This is the period when the tree's growth is most vigorous. A few days after repotting, the new roots will already begin to colonize the pot. After repotting them, put your trees in the shade

every six or seven years will do.

This is not so with a flowering or fruit tree; these must continue to be repotted every year.

8. Repotting an indoor bonsai

For indoor bonsai, repot at the end of spring, towards May or a little bit earlier if the weather has started to turn (hot, long days). A warm location without a draft

destined for the "cascade" style, so as to lower the tree's center of gravity into the pot and keep it from falling over.

6. Repotting

Repotting is routine for a plant that lives in a pot. Eventually, the soil will be spent; it will have nearly disappeared to the benefit of the demanding roots. The signs will be clear: the tree dries out very quickly and seems always to be out of water

to be fastened in the pot. Only its system of rootlets is indispensable to it. Each repotting forces the tree to grow "younger" because all the important roots are eliminated to encourage the regeneration of new rootlets. The eternal vigor of bonsai resides in this.

7. Repotting an outdoor bonsai

Repotting bonsai at the end of fall would make them spend the winter in

for about 10 days, and protect them especially from violent rainstorms, which can strip away all the soil in a single shower.

The frequency of repotting varies according to the age of the tree. The younger it is, the more quickly it grows and the more it needs to grow because it is still forming; at this stage, repot it every two or three years. When it is older, every four or five years is enough. Once it matures,

for about two weeks is perfect for these plants. You can even put your trees in a clear plastic bag with holes, which will act as a greenhouse. Indoor bonsai must be repotted with the same frequency as their outdoor counterparts. With flowering and fruit species, since they do not lose their foliage in winter, you can adopt the same frequency as for the broad-leafed trees.

9. How to proceed

Above all, avoid repotting a soaked tree: its soil must be nearly dry. Begin by making sections with the wire that holds the root clump in the container: cut the aluminum wire that passes at the level of the drainage holes. Then take the tree out of the pot. With bamboo sticks, gently unknot the roots, making two-thirds of the soil fall off. Save only the third of the soil around the trunk. Separate the root system delicately to see if it is in good shape (look under the soil as well). Proceed with pruning, either with root scissors or with pruning shears if the roots are too thick. Be careful, of course, not to cut any vital roots.

Put the finishing touches on the pruning by encouraging the outgrowths, rather than a round or oval shape. They will help the roots develop better in the new soil and you will obtain a pretty clump reduced by two-thirds. Clean the pot with water, dry it well and attach the small pieces of plastic screen (but not with metal) to the interior, at the level of the drainage holes. Then cut a piece of rather thin wire (.04 inch, 1 millimeter thick) two times as long as the pot, which will serve to fasten the tree. Put a little compost at the bottom of the pot, mounded slightly, place the root ball on it, and turn it gently so that the soil penetrates the roots well. Add some compost, using sticks to help you insert the soil into all the cracks. Fasten the last inch of the trunk to the edge of the pot fairly loosely with the wire. Cut the excess length, add more soil, repack it with the help of sticks, and smooth the surface well with a coconut fiber brush. Immerse the pot halfway in a basin of water: the water will rise by capillary action and soak the soil. Then shelter it for a few days. Be careful, give mature reflection to the choice of the pot before repotting. A second repotting risks traumatizing the roots needlessly.

The tree should be placed in the first third of an ordinary pot and in the second third if it is a rectangular or oval pot. In the case of a square or round pot, place it in the middle.

10. Knowing your tools

The tools adapted for bonsai offset the difficulty that you might otherwise have penetrating the heart of the tree without damaging the leaves or branches. They enable you to do very precise work. You will only find them in specialized boutiques, sometimes as complete kits. Be sure to dry them and oil them after use because they rust easily.

Branch scissors are used to cut thin or average branches. The quality of pruning will naturally depend on that of the tools used, but also on the care that you take to use them only for cuts of a certain diameter.

Root scissors allow you to divide the roots covered with soil during repotting. They can become a little blunt from the soil, but they allow a neat and clean cut.

Leaf scissors are less indispensable than the preceding two; nonetheless, they remedy the tedious task of cutting all the leafstalks from a tree. This process, which is not often performed, can also be done with fine dressmaking scissors.

The **concave cutters**, typical of the art of

bonsai, have the unique ability to make a concave cut that the bark fills in as it re-grows. They must be perfectly maintained. You can also use these cutters to eliminate very large roots, being careful that they are almost free of soil in order not to damage the angle of the cut.

Wire cutters are very useful for removing or breaking the wires. They have a tiny cutting angle lengthen your fingers and thus allow you to do very tricky work. They often have a flat part that is very useful during repotting for removing the soil from the pot.

Bamboo sticks are very useful in repotting for loosening the soil and separating the roots very gently; this is not so if they are made of metal.

A **coconut fiber brush** serves to smooth the surface of the soil after which is imported from Japan, dries in the open air, so keep the box tightly closed. Be careful: avoid using grafting putty. It does not fall off—it remains stuck to the trunk permanently.

11. Choosing the fertilizer

A bonsai is a tree in full health and it needs to be well fed. The only fertilizer that truly suits it is solid fertilizer made in centimeters), place 8 to 10 balls of fertilizer in it.

12. Applying the fertilizer

Age does not influence the need of trees for fertilizer, but a tree still growing should be fed more than a mature one. The fertilizer must be applied from April to October (for pines, from the end of July to the end of October), on average once a month,

and round edges that prevent the bark from being damaged. Do not try to replace them with classic cutting pliers. You will damage your bonsai. Similar smaller ones are made for miniature bonsai.

Common pliers can very well be those from your toolbox. But it is better if they do not have a pointed angle so as to avoid injuring the tree.

Large defoliation tweezers are indispensable. In effect, they repotting, but before watering.

Cut paste is indispensable. Use it to seal the least little cut. When applied immediately after the cut is made, the putty helps the wound to close. Moisten your fingers before taking a little bit, knead it to soften it, and put it on the wound. Then, with your finger still a little moist, spread it well. Once the bark is healed, the putty will fall off by itself. This product, Japan. Fairly moderate in price, it comes in two sizes: 500 grams or 1 kilo (1 pound or 2 pounds). The latter quantity is sufficient to feed at least 50 trees for a year. It is composed of a flour of soybean oil, fish, or animal scraps (horns, blood, etc.), kneaded and compacted into small balls. If your tree is in a pot of 6 to 8 inches (15 to 20 centimeters) in diameter, use 4 balls. If your pot measures from 12 to 16 inches (30 to 40 because it disintegrates fairly quickly. According to tradition, feeding a tree well at the end of the summer encourages the trunk to thicken. The fertilizer is always placed midway between the trunk and the pot. You can fix it in this spot with a small U in the wire stuck in the soil or put it in a small mesh basket from the market. This keeps it from attracting flies, especially after a heavy rain or in the heat. Indoors, to reduce the unpleasant odor, you can press the small balls of fertilizer into the soil and cover them carefully. Once every two weeks or so, you might give your indoor bonsai a little fertilizer for "young flowering houseplants" as a complement to the fertilizer balls. It is less rich in nitrogen. Be careful, give fertilizer only to trees whose leaves are adult; otherwise you risk burning

of their leaves. Therefore, they must feel the cold, and the less you bring them in, the better. Adequate light exposure is crucial to shorten the internodes. Add to this just the right amount of water and the foliage of your trees will very naturally tend to shrink. Elevate your bonsai around 36 to 40 inches (90 to 100 centimeters) off the ground to keep away small hands or

always offer the most favorable position. Try to choose species that can flourish in the conditions you will offer them. The north is the least favorable exposure for the good development of bonsai; it offers very little sunlight in the spring. Conifers especially cannot survive there. However, it suits broad-leafed shade trees—the Japanese maple or azalea, for

The exigencies of summer (shade) and winter (shelter) are paramount. These safeguards must always be in place. And plan for a water reserve near your bonsai, such as a large clay bowl, to maintain the water's optimal temperature.

14. Where to place your indoor bonsai

Here again, needs vary according to the season. Tropical, or indoor, trees

the leaves and stopping their growth. Also, never fertilize a flowering tree or one in the process of making fruit because you will make them fall.

13. Where to place your outdoor bonsai

Outdoor trees need sunlight, wind, and rain; keeping them indoors will inevitably cause their death. Furthermore, they need to have a true winter rest, a pause in plant growth with the fall

pets. Be especially careful to fasten the pots to the shelf; a fall is a catastrophe, whether caused by earthquake, wind, or carelessness. Remember that wind is a particular hazard for bonsai kept outdoors. In choosing their placement, carefully consider sun exposure as it changes through the seasons. This can be much more difficult indoors than out in the garden. Balconies and windowsills do not

example—very well. Southern and western exposures are good for just about all species, provided you remember to plan for shade in the summer. The east suits all the broad-leafed trees as well as the juniper. In winter, though, be careful of the very first rays of morning which can be rather hot; they could accelerate the development of buds and cause considerable damage.

do not experience a true winter, simply a period of repose. In their native habitat, this corresponds to higher humidity associated with slightly lower temperatures. In the more northern latitudes, winter means the trees must be brought back in from their outdoor summer idyll. The change may cause them to suffer from dryness in the air and a lack of light, so choose a well-lit place for them, perhaps next to a window, but a good distance from any heat source. A summer rest outdoors is ideal. Barring that, try to place them in front of a window facing east. They will benefit from the morning sun. On the other hand, avoid a western or southern exposure entirely, where your trees risk being cooked. If you only have the north to offer, try to place them in front of a

month," whether growing, blooming, or forming its fruit.

The art is in giving it water only when it is thirsty. For this reason, it is believed in Japan that it takes a student (of bonsai) five years to learn how to water. The hardest part is actually to be there when the tree is thirsty. Not only that, knowing exactly how much water to give requires great sensitivity.

foliage and gently waters the soil. This is lot easier for outdoor bonsai than for indoor ones.

The majority of bonsai lovers have recourse to the sink. They immerse the tree in water for a few minutes—not necessarily completely, but at least all of the pot—until it has stopped making bubbles, proof that it is well soaked. Let the tree drain for a few minutes afterwards.

ing with an old toothbrush, and be very careful.

So as to prevent this buildup and because the majority of plants treated as bonsai are acid loving, soft water is a virtual necessity, for both watering and misting. Calcium makes unsightly deposits on the leaves which are difficult to remove.

In Japan, there is no calcium in the tap water

large bay window. If you live in a place with low light, artificial light, even year round, is an acceptable substitute; they require from 12 to 14 hours per day on average.

15. Watering
This is the only absolutely indispensable daily task. Just like us, a tree is not thirsty at the same time every day. It depends on the season, its placement, its age, and its "time of the

When a tree has drunk too much, its leaves will begin to "stick their noses in the air." In the case of a pine tree, the needles begin to turn brown. This is to be avoided at all cost. Each tree must dry out according to the needs of its species and its individual situation.

The best way to water your trees is to sprinkle them thoroughly with a watering can with a fine spray nozzle: the fine and delicate drizzle rinses the

16. Favoring the water quality
Water quality is crucial, with rainwater being the ideal. The calcium in hard water will have little effect in the short run, but in the long run it forms a thin layer between the edge of the pot and the base (*nebari*) of the tree. And while it is possible to clean the pot with a scrubber, it is nearly impossible to eliminate the calcium deposit on the trunk. Start with gentle brush-

so the problem doesn't exist. Elsewhere, rainwater is probably the best solution; the hard part is collecting it. Other options may be bottled distilled water, aquarium suppliers, and filters such as Brita.

17. Adapting to its needs
According to the season, the water needs of bonsai vary. In winter, protected from the wind, the cold, and the air out there, broad-leafed trees

drink almost nothing. Evergreens need a little more, in general requiring water once a week, except if it freezes: in that case, do not water. Wait until the temperature rises above freezing.

If the cold persists too long, as can sometimes happen, put your trees in a cool well-lit place. Indoor bonsai must receive artificial light from 12 to 14 hours per day; this both prevents their leaf fall and allows them to enjoy a fairly regular watering schedule. On average, watering once or twice a week is good for tropical bonsai, except for the *Ficus*, which must dry out a little more.

From the time that the buds first open in the spring, trees require daily attention and very careful watering—one beautiful, sunny day and a little breeze can totally dry them out.

As the leaves come out, the need increases. Flowering trees must never lack for water; from the time the fruits are formed you should redouble your watch. Be sure to check morning and evening, knowing that the trees must also dry out a little. Conversely, begin to accustom the *Pinus pentaphylla* (or *Parviflora*) or *Pinus thunbergii* to a lack of water so that they make smaller needles. The spring can be extremely rainy, and although an excess of water can be less damaging than a serious slip of mind, days and days of rain may prove traumatic for the trees, especially for those that have just been repotted. The leaves can turn black and may even rot. At that point, it is best to put them under a shelter outside and wait for the soil to dry again before subjecting them

to further bad weather. Indoor bonsai respond to the lengthening days by developing buds, which entails an increased need for water, and so more frequent watering. In the summer, the foliage is adult and therefore, the tree's water needs are more stable. But the dryness of the air means that they must be misted very often. It is absolutely imperative, during this season, to pay attention to the watering. In the case of extreme heat (above 80°F, 27°C), water morning and evening, especially the broad-leafed trees. As for the pines, they must always be thirsty but be careful, at the same time, not to kill them. Water them in the morning and compensate for decreased water by very thorough misting on top of and under the leaves. Conifers have

the ability to absorb atmospheric humidity. At this time, your trees must be in a sunshade, a light screen that protects them from excess sun and wind. This is the bonsai's worst enemy. Horticulturists estimate that the loss of water by evaporation due to the wind can reach as high as 70%, meaning that only 30% of the water given is available to the tree. To compensate for this evaporation, mist routinely.

It is still good practice to arrange your bonsai on a plate layered with moist sand or on bricks themselves placed over a large plate of water. The ideal is for indoor bonsai to spend the summer in the shade outside, being sure to acclimate them gradually to the changed environment. The *Ficus* appreciates full sunlight after a gradual adjustment, and reacts like

outdoor bonsai in its need for water.

In the fall, as the nights begin to cool, the dew covers the colored leaves, and the bonsai have less need for water. Even so, be watchful: there can still be fairly hot, sunny, windy days. This is a pleasant season with few worries—even the pine trees have the right to drink without restraint.

From the time that the have some formidable enemies.

The worst are spider mites. These tiny creatures suck the sap from the leaves, making them fade and take on a yellowish tint before falling. They spin a kind of web on the undersides of the leaves. By the time you become aware of them, it is often too late. Use a product made specifically for them. Spray it on top of cotton of 1/16 inch (2 or 3 millimeters) and the winged aphid (the female installs itself under the leaves peacefully to suck the sap, releasing sticky honeydew).

Their ravages are less grave than those caused by spider mites, but they too must be treated immediately with a product made specifically for them. Outdoor bonsai are commonly

19. Placing outdoor bonsai in the right spot

Outdoor bonsai can be happy in an unheated greenhouse or on a veranda, or even in a garden shelter with a large window. Be careful not to place them to the south or east—there is nothing worse than a sudden change of temperature; a situation to the north is far better. If cold becomes a danger,

first leaves fall, watch that the trees are not too moist. When the need for water lessens, the covering of moss on the outside of the pots might start to encroach dangerously. In case of too frequent showers, be quick to protect them.

18. Combating parasites

Examined and admired as they are each day, bonsai enjoy attention known by few other plants. Even so, they and under the leaves, as well as on the trunk, according to the manufacturer's directions. Treat neighboring plants as well. You can also fill a bucket and immerse only the foliage in it, repeating the process twice a week. Spider mites prefer a dryer atmosphere. Outdoors they often attack hornbeams, elms, and quinces.

Other enemies include the mealy bug (it resembles a ball of snow or prey to aphid attacks. A population of such pests can develop at a frightening rate. Use a commercial product made specifically for them or spray with a concoction of diluted cigarette tobacco.

Slugs can do significant damage outdoors. They enjoy fertilizer and they feast on leaves. FYI: they typically hide during the day in the drainage holes of the pot. cover your shelter with a layer of plastic bubble wrap or a blanket. It is better to leave the trees in complete darkness for a while than to expose them to intense cold. Give them air as soon as possible. Take advantage of a day with temperatures above freezing to open the shelter halfway. The confinement is not good for the trees; it encourages root rot and the growth of moss on the pots. Check your trees at least once a week to water them, remove the dead leaves, and turn them towards the light. As soon as the night temperatures are higher than 39°F (4°C), you can put them back outside.

However, be alert for cold fronts; they are a real threat to very tender leaves.

night temperatures approach 50°F (10°C). Their two main enemies are the dryness of the air and the lack of light, which cause the leaves to fall significantly. To preserve humidity, avoid putting them near a heat source and keep them on a plate full of moist sand or gravel. Sit back and watch the roots find the source through the drainage holes of the pot. Mist them once or

horticultural lamps available at moderate cost—they diffuse light quite comparable to that of the sun. Used with a timer, they will assure the 12 to 13 hours of light necessary for your tropical plants in the depths of winter. If you air out the room, remember to put your tropical bonsai somewhere else; they cannot endure the brutal drop in temperature.

before enclosing them in a clear plastic bag inside a second plastic bag. If you limit yourself to a single bag, the water will condense on the inside of the sack but will not water the tree's soil, which will end up drying out. Indoor bonsai can remain in their usual place, while outdoor ones should be placed in front of a window facing north in an unheated room.

20. Misting indoor bonsai in the winter

Indoor bonsai often come from regions where the winter is mild and very humid and they can live outside all year. For all that, they can still pass an agreeable winter indoors without your having to transform your home into a greenhouse. If they have been outside all summer, bring your trees in a few days before you turn on the heater, or as soon as the

twice a day, under and on top of the leaves (indoor bonsai predators hate ambient humidity, and it is easier to prevent than to get rid of spider mites).

21. Giving them enough light in the winter

Providing adequate light is tricky when you have radiators at window level. If this is the case for you, plan to have an artificial light source. There are so-called

22. Going away

In principle, a bonsai should be checked on daily. This is hard when you go out of town. However, in the winter, they can suffer the neglect for as long as two weeks—at least in the case of outdoor bonsai. And in the summer or fall, an absence of three or four days is not a serious problem. Simply water the bonsai carefully the day of your departure and let them drain

In the spring, the very tender foliage of outdoor bonsai can rot in a plastic bag; so enclose only the pot in a plastic bag and put the tree indoors facing north. Water your bonsai thoroughly, of course, upon returning. Place the outdoor ones in half-shade one or two days before putting them back in their usual place; this is the time it takes for them to re-accustom themselves.

Indoor bonsai used to

living in a stable environment will tolerate your absences much better than those that live outside all year, as the conditions there are unpredictable.

23. Taking your bonsai with you

Some bonsai fanatics take their trees with them everywhere they go. But be careful, they do not transport easily. To withstand trips, they

windows either; you may subject your tiny trees to a veritable tornado.

24. Boarding your bonsai

Without being too fanatical, it is still possible to leave town for several days without a guilty conscience. Certain specialized boutiques and nurseries will board your bonsai. This is an excellent

which, if it is not cut regularly, will quickly grow to its normal size. The first leaves of a shoot are small, and in general, it is only the first leaf, at most the second, that is kept. If your tree is young and you wish to make the trunk grow, just let the new shoot grow. As soon as it has finished its growth, prune it with a pair of leaf scissors. On the other hand, if

which are indispensable to the renewal of branches. Whether they are broad-leafed trees such as the *Ficus* or *Serissa* or conifers such as the *Podocarpus*, indoor bonsai undergo the exact same pruning as their outdoor counterparts. Certain conifers do have a different pruning method. Young juniper shoots, as well as those of the *Pinus pentaphylla*,

must be arranged on plates, covered with a layer of plastic bubble wrap or moss to prevent the pots from banging together and being damaged. In the car, place them on the back seat, protected from the sun's rays by a tissue or mosquito netting. Do not park in full sunlight; the heat this generates can kill plants just as quickly as children and pets. Do not seek to compensate for this by rolling down your

solution if you do not have a friend competent in these things. Above all else, inform yourself about the place where you will leave your trees. Go out of your way to gather a maximum of information and choose a business known for its competency and long-time experience.

25. Maintenance pruning

A bonsai is not a dwarf tree but a shrunken one

your bonsai is mature, prune it immediately, almost to the heart of the bud itself, so that only the first leaf remains. If you fail to do this, the tree will grow full of leaves at the edges and bald in the center and the branches run the risk of dying. With good pruning, light and air penetrate to the very heart of the tree. Its foliage is in harmony with its size, dense and favorable to the growth of new buds,

are pinched with the fingers to keep a third at most. For the *Pinus thunbergii,* the method is different because spring pruning entails the reduction of needles.

26. Shrinking the needles of a pine tree

The only true difficulty in the cultivation of pine trees as bonsai is maintaining their miniature foliage, getting them to make small needles. In Japan, the summer heat and humidity are such that enthusiasts can allow themselves to cut the shoot, or "candle" completely from the *Pinus thunbergii* or the *Pinus densiflora*, which causes the appearance of lateral buds. At this stage, only a third of a single shoot is kept. It is this one that will carry the tufts of adult needles, which are necessarily smaller as the tree is worn out

ment. You will surely sin by excess, but it is better to water too much than not enough. In the end, you run only the risk of having the needles a little longer than desired, which is preferable to the loss of the tree. To compensate for the soil's dryness, mist frequently. Pine trees easily absorb atmospheric humidity through their foliage. Towards the end of July,

27. Renewing the foliage of outdoor bonsai

Obtaining small leaves or small needles calls for particular techniques. Certain species, like maples or *Zelkova*, renew their foliage fairly easily. These trees have an extremely vigorous growth. The spring shoots are long and full of life, and the leaves that come from them are often enormous with

two weeks, the buds will begin to grow, and a new foliation will appear. Obviously, withhold all fertilizer during this period. You will thus force trees worn out by their first foliation to make a second round of very small leaves with tiny internodes.
Be careful: because this pruning is exhausting, only trees that have been repotted over a

from growing the second shoot. In more northern climates, it is difficult to remove the first shoot completely because it is generally not hot or humid enough. The summer is too short for a second generation of shoots to mature into needles. So it is better to pinch the shoot with your fingers, keeping only a third of it, and using thirst to force smaller needles. Only experience can teach the perfect treat-

when the foliage has reached its adult size, give a thorough application of fertilizer, and remove all solid fertilizer residue before the beginning of spring. From September to around mid-October, the two-year-old needles will turn yellow and fall. This is normal (in fact, remove them yourself from time to time if nature doesn't do it for you).

internodes immoderately long—in brief, a nightmare for bonsai enthusiasts. The solution is simple. Prune the tree normally, keeping only the first pair of leaves, then towards the end of April or the beginning of May when the leaves have reached their adult form, cut all the leafstalks. Remove all the leaves this way and take this time to prune all the branches that have grown too long with the initial growth. In around

year earlier and are in perfect health can endure it. As soon as the leaves are adult, fertilize it. Conifers will not survive this process, but you can get a similar result with skillful watering.

28. Renewing the leaves of a *Ficus*

A single indoor bonsai, the *Ficus*, undergoes a treatment similar to that of the outdoor bonsai, but for somewhat different reasons. After a winter spent indoors, the leaves become a little "lazy" and often too large.

The following method to make it renew its foliage is popular in Taiwan. All supplies of fertilizer must be suspended during this period of foliage renewal.

In mid-June, cut all the leaves to the level of the leafstalk and prune all the edges of the buds before enclosing the producing very small leaves. At the same time, space out the watering to induce some dryness and mist it a lot. In less than one month, it will be covered with small, tender green leaves that will change to dark green once they become adult. Prune to only one or two of them. This will encourage the growth of new buds and will force your bonsai foliage to remain dense.

reflection, unless the solution seems obvious to you.

Here, the time spent watering can serve you well. From this, you will have been able to "develop an eye for your tree," you will have learned to look, to know the strengths and flaws of your tree. After each pruning remember to seal the wounds with cut paste.

helped to curve the branches. It took a very long time and gave fairly uncertain results. These days, wrapping the branch with aluminum or copper wire of a diameter adapted to that of the branch gives a perfect result in minutes. Copper wire is suitable for conifers, aluminum for broad-leafed trees. The copper is made supple by heating it before placing it on the

Ficus in a plastic bag—which will act as a greenhouse—for one or two weeks, depending on the heat. The leafstalks will turn yellow, then fall, and in less than two weeks, the tree will regain small, very tender buds.

At this stage, put your bonsai outside if you can. Pierce the plastic sack; the tree will gradually get used to the outside air. Place it in full sun, which will cause it to react by

29. Shape pruning

Unlike other pruning to maintain the shape and beauty of your bonsai, shape pruning is to give it an overall shape. It means cutting the branches, often the main ones. This process is not benign and you should begin by observing your tree from all angles, while keeping a certain number of rules in mind: your bonsai must form a triangle, the arrangement of the branches is crucial, etc. Take time for

30. Wiring

After having pruned your tree to shape, it is logical to wire it to give it the desired curve. This technique became popular towards the end of the Second World War; copper and aluminum wire have enabled a veritable revolution. For centuries, the Chinese method prevailed. It consisted of using hemp strings between the branches to bring them together. Weights

tree. Copper will become dark brown as it hardens. Aluminum is gentle and does not wound the fragile bark of broad-leafed trees. The wire is placed neither too tightly nor too loosely at regular intervals. Once it is in place, you can give the branch the angle you desire. If the wire seems too large, wrap it with raffia or paper so as not to wound the bark. Normally, the branches must appear at the outside of a curve, never at the inside. Be careful, wire is not intended to remain on the tree for very long. The wood of broad-leafed trees grows very quickly and is susceptible to scarring by the end of three weeks or a month, especially if you put the wire on just before spring. On a conifer, it can remain in place from six to ten months. Check it regularly because bark

when the tree is in full growth, in May or June: the healing is more rapid and the foliage is easily renewed.

31. Making the trunk grow

It is satisfying to the eye to have a certain thickness to the trunk. To arrive at it, try to choose a branch if possible in the "back" of the tree, which will not be pruned for several

paste to the cut. Do not use fertilizer since the healing is not totally done and don't forget to repot every year. Naturally, during this time continue pruning your tree normally. For a bonsai still growing, do this project in the ground in a vegetable garden. But if you leave its branches or its trunk wired, check regularly every two or three days that marks are not

mountains of Hokkaido, the most northern island of Japan, where climatic conditions are very harsh. The trees there grow small and sickly, tortured by wind, snow and ice. A true bonsai mine! Despite prodigious care by the professionals, it was necessary to uproot quantities of trees to obtain a single surviving one. There came a time when Japanese authorities

marked by a wire remains so for life. There is no way to remedy this flaw. And a marked tree loses a significant part of its value, esthetic as well as monetary.
Just like shape pruning, wiring is done in the winter when the trees have no leaves. Pines are also shaped at this time when the old needles have fallen and the buds are not yet active. To the contrary for tropical trees, such as the *Ficus*— it is better to proceed

seasons. It will thus grow and greatly surpass the size of your tree. At the same time, the trunk is also growing. Be sure to repot every year because the main root will grow too, often to the detriment of the others, laying waste to your efforts to grow balanced, harmonious surface roots. When you judge the trunk to be thick enough, cut this last branch, called the "sacrifice branch," to the base, and apply cut

forming on the bark. Generally, the ground is reserved for the production of fairly large bonsai, which on average spend two or three years there to obtain a very fat trunk, and only a trunk. All the work of "sculpting" the bonsai will be done once it is put in the pot.

32. Obtaining a "deadwood"

At one time, bonsai nursery workers went out on expeditions in the

decided to prohibit this practice. Today, except with permission from the owner of the land where the tree is growing, you cannot take it. This *Yama-dori* (literally, "mountain road,") was not only a very lucrative activity for rural inhabitants, but truly an art. This process consisted of creating foliage from branches around the trunk or dead branches polished and whitened by the wind. The canons of beauty are identical to those governing bonsai, in general, but with the difference of revealing the living part that brings the sap to the branches.

33. Starting with a young tree

To obtain the same result on a young tree, choose the branch, when shape pruning, that you would like to see treated as "dead-wood." For this, make a

The Japanese use a bright yellow product with a lime sulfur base to protect the "dead branch," or *djin*. It smells very strong, turns white in a few days, and prevents parasite or fungal attacks. To obtain a dead or mutilated trunk, you must literally sculpt it. This is practiced on fat nursery specimens whose base, and only the base, is interesting—with a

only possibility is grafting by approach. Let a branch grow for an entire season, then the following spring, before the leaves have appeared, make a cut in the trunk, at the place where you would like to create a branch. Wire it in a very loose way that will serve as a graft and put it in the cut. Remove some bark equivalent to the diameter of the branch to be grafted,

trunk right through with a drill and forcing the very thin trunk of a young plant of the same species through it. This is done in the spring. In several months, the shoot will have made the trunk of the graft grow, and that of the stock. Presumably, the graft will have taken. Certain bonsai lovers push refinement to the limit: they cut a branch of the tree carrying the future

deep incision all around the bark to circumscribe the "dead" part. Then, with the help of pliers, mince the bark after having cut the thin branches, so as to save only the spirit of the branch. Gently peel off the bark. A few weeks outdoors will serve to bleach it white.

This process is traditionally done on conifers, whose wood is particularly resistant, because that of broad-leafed trees rots fairly quickly.

profusion of knots and spread-out branches. Proceed little by little in carrying out the process over two to three weeks to avoid making the tree suffer needlessly.

34. Creating a branch

It sometimes happens during the shaping of a bonsai, that you deplore the crucial absence of a branch in a spot important to the harmony of the tree. To overcome this natural flaw, the

and plaster the graft immediately on the stock with the help of a thumbtack or a small nail planted firmly in the center. Carefully coat with cut paste or grafting wax. Ideally, this graft should not be overly thick and should almost completely fill in the trunk. Wait at least one year before separating it from the branch that holds it. You have your branch! There is another method too: it consists of piercing the

branch to prevent its bearing leaves with autumnal colors earlier or later than the rest of the tree.

35. Choosing what variety of bonsai to make

Every plant and every tree can be shaped into a bonsai, but not all will necessarily be beautiful. The ideal plant must have naturally small leaves, short internodes, thin branches and wood of ideal hardness and flexibility…unless it is a *Kusa-mono*, or shrunken grass.

For these reasons, oaks and sycamores are very rarely treated as bonsai. Conversely, hornbeams, maples, and pine trees all lend themselves well to the treatment. All methods are good for obtaining the plant that you want to shape into a bonsai, but certain species will be easier to find than others. The found as seeds, or can only be propagated this way. Still others must be sown to produce an attractive base. This is the case with the *Zelkova* and the Thunberg pine. And there is undeniable pleasure in sowing the seed and seeing your tree sprout. Whether you buy your seeds or collect them, they must spend the winter in coolness and humidity. It aware that seeds from the same packet can grow at different rates.

37. Propagation by cuttings

Very classic, and quicker than sowing, this is the most used method of propagation, notably for tropical (indoor) bonsai. Whether for cuttings or for trees, the process is the same. The only difference is that tropical plants must be propa- cuttings in a clear plastic bag, and place this in the light, but not directly in the sun. Two to three weeks later, the cuttings that have taken will have kept their leaves, the others will have turned black and rotted. Clean them (to prevent fungal or other infection). As soon as all the new leaves appear, pierce the sack that serves as a "greenhouse" so that air can penetrate it. This

Pyracantha and the hawthorn, for instance, can be found at any nursery. And *Serissa* and *Stewartia* will be more difficult to find.

36. Propagation by sowing

Obviously, you will obtain a finished bonsai more rapidly by beginning with adult "material." By beginning with a seed, you will need, on average, twice as long as with a young plant. But certain species are only is simplest to sow them in a pot and let them spend the winter in the same conditions as your outdoor bonsai. In the case of tropical bonsai, wait for spring to sow; such seeds often have a very short life span. For sowing, proceed in the same manner as for standard potting, using your usual compost. But only cover the seed with the equivalent of its height in soil if you want it to germinate well. Water and wait. Be gated in the heat. As with pruning, gather stems of 4 inches (10 centimeters) with "matured" wood that has become dark. Only these cuttings will have a chance to root. Keep only two or three solid, hard leaves. Cut the end or the tender terminal buds, and stick them two-thirds of the way in a bonsai mixture with 40 to 50% added horticultural sand. Water the soil well before putting the pot containing your will enable your plants to adjust and gain strength before confronting the open air. Proceed slowly, over two weeks or so.

38. Layering

More than a method of propagation, this is a convenient means to make a branch take root and it allows you to reshape the surface roots.

Just before the end of spring, remove a half inch (one centimeter) of bark from all around the branch that you want to take root. Fashion a light insulating layer of leaf compost, if possible mixed with moss to humidify it, and apply it all around the part with the bark removed. Enclose the whole thing in an opaque plastic bag, tie it at the bottom, water thoroughly, then tie it at the top. If you first put a clear bag, then another opaque

take the tree you want. Go looking for your tree at the end of November, or at the beginning of March, if you must. Separate the roots, being careful to save as much soil as possible around the main root, in order to preserve the precious rootlets. Surround it with moss and water. Take care especially during transport not to break up the soil. Put the tree back in

40. Using young plants (*Yama-dori*)

By extension, *Yama-dori* is used to indicate young plants. Certain nurseries specialize in them, but you can find them everywhere. The choice is vast, the price modest but variable, according to the rarity of the species. Make the effort to choose them yourself because it is the shape that will guide you. Even if wiring allows you to

notably one in the back, which is very important for balance. At the end of four or five years, it will be worthy of repotting in a bonsai pot. To make the trunk grow, around the fourth year, let the head "run its course" for one or two years: a good pruning, and its lateral branch will then replace the crown.

one, you will see the roots appear at the end of two or three months. When the sack is covered with roots, cut under the leaf compost insulation and plant it. You have your new tree.

39. Collecting in the wild (*Yama-dori*)

Yama-dori, that is, collecting in the forest, is forbidden. On the other hand, if you have permission from the land's owner, you can

the ground as quickly as possible, sheltered from the sun and wind. For two or three years, treat this tree as a seriously ill patient in convalescence. Only at the end of this time can you repot it in a very large pot. A few years later, the pot will become that of a bonsai. Modify the tree's appearance very gradually in small steps in order not to traumatize it. A bonsai that comes from *Yama-dori* renders untold satisfaction.

do what you want, you will save a lot of time by letting yourself be guided by the innate qualities of the tree. A young plant that already has its first branch, a crown and beautiful surface roots is a great start. To force it to branch out, you need only cut its top. Repotted in a cultivation pot with the roots plastered over a shard of terra cotta, the tree will grow its secondary branches in two years,

Conclusion

Buying or making a bonsai yourself, maintaining it with care and skill: we have seen that all the art of bonsai is in the following of sometimes vague rules. The *story* has presented to you the origin and the development of this art. The *portraits* have allowed you to understand better the unique qualities of the species that you will most often encounter. The *Keys to Success* have given you the tools to answer questions you will have.

With this work, I hope to have shared with you my passion and the means to satisfy it fully. One last thing: remember that it is not enough to master the technique—you must also love the plants. Perhaps even more than for other plants, you must be their master and their caretaker and companion. This is your mission.

[Index]

[Glossary]

To understand some botanical words better

Acidic: this is said of soil whose pH is less than 7. From 1 to 7, the soil is suitable for heath peat plants. Above this threshold, only plants that can stand calcium will survive.
Broad-leafed: see deciduous.
Chokkan: formal upright.
Deciduous: a plant that loses all its foliage in the winter.
Defoliation: process consisting of cutting all the leaves from a tree to force it to make new ones.
Dioecious: a species that needs a male and a female plant to produce fruit.
Djin: all branches or extremities of branches stripped, and turned white by bad weather.
Evergreen: a plant that does not lose its leaves or needles in the winter.
Fukinagashi: very ethereal, light shape, said to be "literate." It is sometimes compared to the "windswept" shape.
Ishitsuki: the tree is either totally planted in a rock cavity which becomes its pot, or its roots hug the rock before being planted in the pot.
Kengai: "cascade" shape, the head of the tree is below the level of the pot.
Kusa-mono: "grass in a pot" or "bonsai grass;" miniature bonsai made from herbaceous plants.
Layering: manner of propagation which consists of causing the rooting of a plant part by putting it in contact with the soil, without having separated it from the mother plant.
Ligneous: a plant that produces wood.
Mature: this is said of a young, green, tender and supple shoot, which near the middle of the summer, becomes rigid like wood.
Maintenance pruning: regular pruning done to maintain the shape of the tree.
Moyogi: informal upright shape, a little curved.

Neagari: this is said of a tree whose roots are exposed in a very significant way, either by the caprice of nature or by the nature of the species itself. The *Ficus* is an excellent example.
Nebari: signifies "surface roots."
Propagation by cuttings: reproduction by taking a piece of the plant to make it root.
Repotting: renewing the bonsai's soil without necessarily changing the pot.
Rule of three points: this is a fundamental rule of bonsai. The top, the main branch and second most important branch should form a triangle, from which no branch should stray.
Semi-evergreen: depending on the intensity of the cold, the plant loses some part of its foliage.
Shakan: "slanting" shape, the head of the tree is outside of the pot.
Shaping: to give a shape to a branch or a tree.
Shape pruning: significant pruning to give a shape to the tree.
Sui-seki: literally, "stone of water," "rock artwork" evoking the mountains, waves, and profiles of fantastic animals.
Wintering: period during which the bonsai is sheltered from the bad weather of winter.
Wire: copper wire for conifers or aluminum wire for broad-leafed trees.
Wiring: putting a wire around the trunk or one of the branches to give it a shape.
Yama-dori: literally, "mountain road," means in Japanese, "comes from forest collecting," or collecting in the wild. This term extends to the use of young plants.
Yose-ue: shape of planting "in a forest."

*To respect the will of the author who worked in the concerns of the tradition, the term "bonsai" has been considered invariable and has not taken the plural form.

[Photo Credits]

All photographs are by
Jacques Boulay except for the
following references:
Pages 6,7,9, and 10
Photothèque Hachette,
Pages 22,23,25, and 27
Bruno Delmer,
Pages 35 and 37
Isabel Samson,
Page 33 Beatrice
Pichon-Clarisse,
Page 94 Isabel Samson,
Page 104 (two central images)
Beatrice Pichon-Clarisse,
Page 150 (first two images)
Bruno Delmer.

[Thanks]

Bruno Delmer:
Above all, I am eager to give infinite thanks to Mr. Hideo Kato,
who had the courage to accept for the first time a foreign intern
for a year. With all his family and his other students, he welcomed
me and continues to welcome me as a son. I would also like to
thank Mr. Rémy Samson, thanks to whom I have discovered what
is one of the great joys of my life. A very special thought for Mr.
Auguste Prédour, my main professor at Genech, for his sense of
humor, his patience and his real sense of pedagogy.
Finally, to all my family who are willing to share the life of my
bonsai and to all the numerous friends for whom bonsai rhymes
with passion: Mr. and Ms. Phung from the "Pépinière de Chine,"
Pierre and Danièle Vergnes from "L'arbre de vie," Mr. Alain-
Frédéric Bisson and Mr. Lodder from the Lodder nurseries in
Holland.

Yves le Floc'h and Jacques Boulay warmly thank Mr. and Mrs.
Rémy Samson for their invaluable help throughout the production
of this work.

The mention "Collection: Rémy Samson" which accompanies the
photographs of the trees in the boxes refers to the Rémy Samson
Bonsai nurseries, 25 rue Chateaubriand, 92 290 Châtenay-Malabry.

Jardin des Sens series editior: Yves le Floch'h Soye
Translation: Kelly Ramke

1 3 5 7 9 10 8 6 4 2

Published by Sterling Publishing Company, Inc.
387 Park Avenue South, New York, N.Y. 10016
Originally published in France under the title *Jardin des Sense: Bonsaï*
and © 2000 by Hachette Livre (Hachette Pratique)
English translation © 2002 by Sterling Publishing Co., Inc.
Distributed in Canada by Sterling Publishing
c/o Canadian Manda Group, One Atlantic Avenue, Suite 105
Toronto, Ontario, Canada M6K 3E7
Distributed in Great Britain and Europe by Cassell PLC
Wellington House, 125 Strand, London WC2R 0BB, England
Distributed in Australia by Capricorn Link (Australia) Pty. Ltd.
P.O. Box 704, Windsor, NSW 2756 Australia

Printed in Singapore
All rights reserved

Sterling ISBN 0-8069-7303-X